THIS ISN'T

THE LIFE I

Signed

UP FOR

Bethany House Books
by Donna Partow

DONNA PARTOW

THIS ISN'T THE LIFE I *Signed* UP FOR

BETHANYHOUSE
MINNEAPOLIS, MINNESOTA

Published by Bethany House Publishers
A Ministry of Bethany Fellowship International
11400 Hampshire Avenue South
Bloomington, Minnesota 55438

Printed in the United States of America by
Bethany Press International, Bloomington, Minnesota 55438

ISBN 0-7642-2670-3 (pbk.)

DONNA PARTOW is a Christian communicator with a compelling testimony of God's transforming power. Her uncommon transparency and passion for Christ have been used by God at women's conferences and retreats throughout North America. She is the bestselling author of numerous books and has been a popular guest on more than two hundred radio and TV programs, including *Focus on the Family*.

If your church sponsors an annual women's conference or retreat, perhaps they would be interested in learning more about the author's special weekend programs. She is also available for luncheons and one-day events. For more information, contact:

Donna Partow
Web site: *www.becomingavessel.com*
E-mail: dpartow@cox.net

CONTENTS

I DIDN'T

~~*Sign*~~

UP FOR

THIS LIFE

I Didn't Sign Up for This Life!

I have a recurring nightmare.

I'm in college, sitting down to take a final exam, when I suddenly realize, "Hey, I never signed up for this class!" The exam is on biochemistry or nuclear physics, when I thought I had signed up for basket weaving. What I assumed would be a no-brainer turns into the ultimate test. Everyone else seems to be zipping along, while I stare blankly at the first problem. *They're making it look so easy,* I think to myself. Waves of fear and insecurity sweep over me as the reality dawns that I am completely unprepared.

Sometimes life can feel like that. We suddenly find ourselves faced with a challenging exam—like cancer, a prodigal child, or the loss of a loved one. We want to cry out: "Hey, God, this isn't the life I signed up for! I *specifically remember* signing up for great parents, a great marriage, and great kids who rise up and call me blessed. I signed up for lifelong friendships, thin thighs, and vibrant health. Instead, I find myself in the middle of a life I DIDN'T sign up for.

My husband says he doesn't love me anymore. My daughter just pierced her tongue. The bills are stacked a mile high, and my company just announced another round of layoffs. To top it all off, I'm forty pounds overweight and my doctor says I'm a heart attack waiting to happen."

Can we be honest? Was there ever a time in your life when you said the following prayer: "Dear God, my life is going way too smoothly right now. Could you please arrange for me to get in a car accident so I can suffer from a severe back injury?" Or maybe you've prayed this one: "Thank you, Lord, for allowing me to get pregnant, but do me a favor: complicate the delivery or make sure my child is born with serious health problems."

What? You never prayed those prayers? Do you know anyone who has?

The obvious truth is: No one signs up for the challenges of life. But in the real world, tough times are inevitable. We all want to live "happily ever after." Since you've picked up this book, I'm guessing that, in one way or another, you've encountered a few bumps on the road to bliss. Believe me, I know exactly how you feel.

Is God Trying to Teach Me a Lesson?

I originally planned to title this book *God, Please Don't Teach Me Anything Else . . . I Really Don't Want to Know.* When you're going through tough times, people love to "comfort" you with reassuring words about how it will build your character and how you're learning important life lessons. I want to say, "You know,

I'm pretty content with my character right where it is. And I already know everything I want to know: like how to drive through McDonald's for a vanilla milk shake when someone hurts my feelings and how to avoid working on deadlines by calling my mom. With Oreos in one hand and a chocolate-covered doughnut in the other, I'm prepared to face whatever life can dish out." Are you with me?

I recently shared this life-concept with my spiritual mentor, who was unimpressed. "Now, Donna," she said in a voice usually reserved for the students in her first-grade class. "You know you don't really mean that. You know you want to learn all that God has for you so you can become the person he wants you to be." Then she explained that an easy life is not necessarily a good life and a good life is rarely easy. I know she's right, but wouldn't it be great if there *were* an easier way? Wouldn't you like to get a Ph.D. in the School of Life without ever taking a challenging class? Imagine if you never had to face adversity, never had to make any tough choices. Never had to live with the painful consequences of other people's choices.

In reality, choices are the stuff of life. First you make your choices; then your choices make you. This is how the Bible puts it:

> *First you make your choices; then your choices make you.*

This day I call heaven and earth as witnesses against you that I have set before you life and death, blessings and curses. Now choose life, so that you and your children may live and that you may love the Lord your God, listen to his voice, and hold fast to him. (Deuteronomy 30:19–20)

So, basically, we human beings have to take a multiple-choice exam every day of our lives. It's the same question every time.

While living on earth you can either:

a. Choose life.

b. Choose death.

c. Refuse to make any choices (which is, in itself, a choice).

d. Go back and forth between a. and b.

Of course, while we're taking this particular exam, God is standing there saying, "The correct answer is 'a.' Choose 'a.' Your life will be so much better if you choose 'a.' "

It might seem that life would be easier if God would do the choosing for us. Eve could have passed the first exam with flying colors if God had reached down into the Garden of Eden, grabbed her greedy little fingers, and prevented her from grasping the forbidden fruit. In the same way, God could have prevented your husband from choosing to make his career a higher priority than your family. He could have prevented your teenager from getting into that car with a bunch of drunken friends.

God could have created a world filled with flawless humans who always choose right, but he already had an entire universe teeming with created things that had no choice but to honor him. The stars in the sky *must* obey him and the planets *must* remain in their appointed orbits. The flowers in the field *must* show forth his glory. The oceans *must* proclaim his power and majesty. The birds of the air and the animals that fill the earth *must* illustrate his beauty and creativity. They cannot do otherwise.

We are the only created beings who get to choose how we will respond to God and the world around us. We are the only creatures facing that multiple-choice exam with a pencil in our hand and the power to say, "God, I know what you want me to do, but I'm going to choose the opposite anyway. I'm going with 'b' and you can't stop me." It was a risky move on his part to create humans as free moral agents. God knew that from the beginning, but he willingly opened himself up to the pain of rejection. He is indeed grieved when people choose to disobey and dishonor him, but God doesn't force himself on anyone. I believe he finds more joy in one person who *chooses* to love him—and to keep on loving him even in the face of adversity—than he finds in all the beauty of every other created thing combined.

Perhaps you have experienced a major tragedy. Or maybe you are simply overwhelmed by the accumulated weight of one disappointment after another. You can't always control what happens to you, but you can choose how you will respond. You can say, "This isn't the life I signed up for . . . and I refuse to accept how things have turned out. I'm going to stay stuck in this place of pain forever and no one can stop me." Or you can declare: "This isn't the life I signed up for and I'm absolutely

> **"**
>
> *You can't always control what happens to you, but you can choose how you will respond.*
>
> **"**

heartbroken about it. But I know I have to move forward to find hope and healing. God, please show me the way."

Are You Ready to Get Real?

This is a book for people who want to follow the path to hope and healing. There's only one requirement: You have to be willing to get real. With God. With yourself. With everybody else. I'm telling you right up front: If you like books that give THE definitive answer—neatly packaged and distilled into ten simple steps—you will not like this book. If you like books written by straight-A students who know all the answers, who never blow it, never doubt God, and never struggle, you will not like this book. Repeat: You will not like this book! But if you're willing to enroll in a class taught by a fellow student of life, I welcome you to read along. I think you should know that I've pulled no punches. The test for every sentence was "Is this true in *my own life* . . . or is this a nice platitude that 'ought' to be true? Am I just writing this because it sounds like something Christians are 'supposed to' say?" If it wasn't true *for me*, I didn't write it. As a result, this book is guaranteed to contain 0 percent *oughts* and *shoulds*. Instead, it's 100 percent real life.

> "*This book is guaranteed to contain 0 percent oughts and shoulds. Instead, it's 100 percent real life.*"

Since I'm asking you to be honest, here's an honest confession: I've wasted years of my life arguing with God. I've expended immeasurable time and energy telling him how unfair he was, how unfair the universe was, how life had done me wrong, how everybody else got a fair shake while I got a raw deal. Nothing in my life made sense to me. I resented almost everyone on the planet because I didn't think anyone's suffering could possibly compare with mine. When I met people who had clearly suffered more, I resented them too, because they got more sympathy than me. In case you haven't guessed it by now, I was an emotional wreck.

The hardest part was this: In many ways, I was absolutely right. Life had been unfair to me. I had faced some tough exams. My circumstances were incredibly painful. Significant people in my life had hurt me, and "they" were clearly wrong. I was clearly right. Guess how far "being right" got me? It wasn't until I let go of the need to be right and started pursuing the need to be healed that I found any hope for a better life.

> **"**
> *It wasn't until I let go of the need to be right and started pursuing the need to be healed that I found any hope for a better life.*
> **"**

I can say unequivocally that I am a completely different person today than I was when I set out to write this book a year ago. I don't have all the answers, and I've flunked my share of tests, but I do know one thing for sure: What God has done in my life is nothing short of miraculous. He has transformed me from "The Dead Woman Walking"[1]

---

[1] Believe it or not, this was actually the nickname one of my family members gave me. That's how filled with grief and despair my life was.

into a glorious testimony to the power of Christ's resurrection. I now know, with every fiber of my being, that God can bring new life where there was once nothing but death. If he can breathe life back into my weary heart, mind, and soul . . . there's hope for everyone.

My initial goal in writing *This Isn't the Life I Signed Up For* was simply to offer comfort to women like myself who felt like they'd been mysteriously plopped down into the middle of the wrong life. I had no idea that God was going to give me answers to questions that had baffled me for years. In fact, I had actually come to the place where I didn't believe there were any answers other than "Life is tough. Hold on till you get to heaven." I know differently now.

I know what it feels like to survey your life and conclude, "This isn't the life I signed up for!" At last I have experienced that incredible moment when I can honestly add the phrase, "But I'm finding hope and healing!" God is bringing good out of the pain—much to my astonishment and delight. I am certain he can do the same for you. It is my prayer that you will find hope and healing on the pages of this book. And if you read it with an open heart and mind, I'm confident you will.

I've written a separate Growth Guide[2] to accompany *This Isn't the Life I Signed Up For*, because *working* through this material, as opposed to *reading* through it, can make the difference between being entertained and changing your life. I hope you find this book

---

[2]The Growth Guide is suitable for small groups and includes a leader's guide. Available through your local Christian bookstore or by calling 1-866-241-6733. A companion audiobook is also available.

thought-provoking, stimulating, convicting, and yes, entertaining. But if that's all that happens, I will have failed in my purpose. My purpose is to give you what God has given me: a chance to discover the life you *did* sign up for.

I DIDN'T

Sign

UP FOR A

PAINFUL

CHILDHOOD

CHAPTER TWO

I Didn't Sign Up for a Painful Childhood

It was Veteran's Day. November 11, 2001. I was a guest at a small church in rural Ohio, where I had just finished leading a women's conference. The pastor invited all the veterans to stand up, state their name, branch of service, number of years served, and the military theater they had served in. By the time all the men had spoken, I was weeping uncontrollably. Which wouldn't have been a problem, except that I was scheduled to deliver the morning message. I stood in front of the packed church, struggling to pull myself together, unable to utter a word for several long minutes.

The wars that have shaped modern history have shaped my life too. Just looking at the gray hairs and fragile bodies of the WWII veterans was enough to shake me. They served as an undeniable reminder that my once invincible father—the tough-talking, Harley-riding "man who invented cool"—was no more. He had been transformed before my very eyes into the unthinkable: an old man and a daily reminder that I'm getting older too.

My father was part of the famous 101st Airborne—the Screaming Eagles who dropped out of the skies over Europe, bringing victory wherever they trod. We grew up on WWII movies, and we always imagined my father as the hero in every story. So it was only natural for my oldest brother to volunteer to serve in the Airborne when Vietnam rolled around. He was seventeen years old the day he signed up dreaming of medals—like the Purple Heart my father kept in the nightstand beside his bed. The one we kids would sometimes sneak in to look at when my dad was on the road. It made us feel safe—like we had a hero to protect us.

The medal was the only part of what he signed up for that became a reality for my brother. During his first weeks in Vietnam, he watched 78 of the 80 young men he'd gone through Jump School with get slaughtered in a single battle. The nightmare was just beginning. For him, for our family, for millions of Americans, the Vietnam War was a harrowing ordeal. By the time my brother had completed his tour of duty he was a heroin addict. Before long three of my brothers and one of my sisters were addicted to the drug as well. No one in my family had signed up for heroin addiction, but apparently it had signed up for us. Our whole world was turned upside down as my parents and the rest of us kids tried to make sense of the senseless—tried to retain our sanity in the midst of the insanity.

Somewhere, I got lost in the middle of the mess, and it's taken me a long, long time to get found again. I can't describe what happened to me, but if you've lived through something similar, I don't need to. And if you have never found yourself in a place where *other people's choices* rocked your world, I'm not sure I can capture the powerless feeling that overtakes you.

This isn't the life I signed up for! I wanted to scream. And I did scream it, in a million different ways—none of them healthy or wise, although some were more socially acceptable than others. Because I was so ashamed of the problems in our family, I felt like "the little girl no one was allowed to play with." Rejection haunted my steps. It was almost as if I had emblazoned a sign on my forehead: "Please reject me and get it over with." Emotional pain became a way of life for me. An atmosphere. The air I breathed. The ocean I swam in. The jungle I inhabited—a land of cannibals.

How a Child Grows Up to Become a Cannibal

You know what a cannibal is, right? A cannibal is someone who eats other people. But do you know why cannibals eat other people? It's not for the taste. They do it because they believe the very act of consuming another human being will somehow make them more powerful. Sound familiar? I'm talking about emotional cannibalism here. I'm talking about people who feel the only way they can lift themselves up is by tearing other people down. I'm talking about self-appointed critics, people who know what's wrong with everyone except the person in the mirror. I'm talking about gossips and backbiters.

> **"**
> *A cannibal is someone who eats other people.*
> **"**

I'm talking about myself.

At least that's who I used to be. I didn't sign up to become an emotional cannibal. But I became one anyway. The Scripture says this is a dangerous way to live. "If you keep on biting and devouring each other, watch out or you will be destroyed by each other" (Galatians 5:15). If only more Christians would heed that warning, the local church would be a much safer place for everyone.

The Destructive Seed Planter

Cannibals aren't born; they're made. And nothing breeds cannibals like a painful childhood. Just as God is the Lover of Your Soul—the One who wants to speak life and truth to your heart, you also have an enemy.[1] And I am absolutely convinced that the enemy of your soul comes early. In John 8:44 Jesus said, in speaking of Satan, "When he lies, he speaks his native language, for he is a liar and the father of lies." Now, what does it take to be a father? Especially in today's world, all you have to do is plant the seed and take a hike. (Of course, you may then find yourself on the Montel Williams show being publicly subjected to a paternity test . . . but that's a whole different point.) I think that's exactly the kind of father Satan is. He plants his seed and takes a hike. Then the world comes along, waters it, and the seed begins to grow. The lie takes on a life of its own.

---

[1]When I use the term "enemy" I am not referring to Satan personally. He can only be in one place at a time, so the chance that he is personally attacking you at any given moment is quite remote. Instead, I am referring to that legion of fallen angels who work to advance his agenda.

Satan isn't stupid. He knows the earlier he plants his seed, the deeper it will take root and the more difficult it will be to uproot later. He also knows that the most powerful truth in the universe is that we have a loving heavenly Father. That's why he works overtime whispering in the ears of child molesters, goading them on in their filthy work. He knows our image of the Father is marred by our image of earthly fathers—or any male authority figure. Is it any wonder that some estimates show one in four girls is sexually molested before the age of eighteen? The liar is behind it. The destructive seed planter is behind it.

Now, this is important to keep in mind: Just as God chooses to work on the earth through human beings, the enemy does the same. He always chooses a tool—a human being through whom to sow his seed. And he always watches for an opportune moment to act. Perhaps the tool was your mother. And the moment was the day when you came home after being brutally

> **"**
>
> *The most powerful truth in the universe is that we have a loving heavenly Father.*
>
> **"**

picked on at school *again*. You had reached your limit. You needed to know for sure that you mattered to someone, that you really were a lovable human being. But no one told your mom that on Thursday, October 15, 1975, at 4:00 P.M., she needed to forget about making the casserole for the Ladies' Bible Study and focus her attention entirely on you. She didn't know this was going to be a pivotal moment in your emotional development. But the enemy knew, so he blew up the oven and arranged a few irritating phone calls that afternoon. That's why your mom started screaming at you about "socks on the floor" the minute you walked through the door. That's why you were sent to your room rather than cuddled in the rocking chair.

You see, it wasn't about your mom. She never intended to fail you when you needed her most. Your mom wasn't your enemy. Satan was—and is—your enemy. He is the originator of all human suffering.

Maybe you're sitting there thinking, "Who is she kidding? My mother failed me every day of my life. My father completely abandoned me. It wasn't just one moment; it was every moment. My entire childhood is a painful blur." If your parents inflicted pain of that magnitude, you can be certain they did so because they were in tremendous pain of their own. Only hurting people can systematically hurt other people. People in pain inflict the most pain on people they are supposed to love.

That doesn't justify their actions, and it doesn't diminish the damage done, but it takes away some of the sting when you realize it wasn't personal. It wasn't about you. Their actions say *nothing* about your worth as a human being. Instead, they speak volumes about the brokenness of the one(s) who failed you. I sometimes hear adults say, "My parents just didn't love me." Yet ask that same person, "Do you love your children?" and they answer, "Of course I do! What a ridiculous question." Then ask them, "Well, do you personally know anyone who doesn't love their children?" The response: "Well, no, but . . ." But nothing! With very few exceptions, parents love their children. Now, whether they are capable of effectively demonstrating that love is a different matter entirely. But it should come as some comfort to realize that your parents almost certainly DID love you. They just didn't know how to show it.

The Seed in Full Bloom

As long as you continue to buy into the lie, you'll be vulnerable to the schemes of the Destructive Seed Planter. He will be able to exert a negative influence on your behavior and consequently, to a large extent, your destiny. As long as you believe the lie, you'll live like a cannibal.

In an effort to motivate you to let go of the lie, let me show you a cannibal in action and see if you recognize yourself. Let's imagine that Denise and Sue go out to lunch to talk about plans for the upcoming ladies' retreat. Now, unbeknown to Sue, Denise is secretly a cannibal, and poor unsuspecting Sue has no idea that *she is on the menu*. Some time between the minestrone soup and the chicken Caesar salad, Denise turns to Sue and says, "I really hope you're not planning to sing again this year. I've got to be honest with you: Your solo last year really fell flat. I'm thinking my daughter could do something more upbeat and, you know, contemporary." Denise spends the remainder of the luncheon bragging on her daughter. (God help her daughter if she fails to give Denise something to brag about . . . but I'm getting ahead of myself.)

Now, Sue has a couple options here. Option #1: Let it go. She can say to herself, "Well, that's just Denise. I know she's overcome some tough obstacles in her life. She doesn't mean to hurt people when she says stuff like that. She's just desperate to be the center of attention all the time. It's really a shame, because I know she loves God and wants to make a difference. I need to pray for her. Maybe God can use me to bring about some healing in her life."

Of course, Sue can only respond with that kind of compassion if she's dealt with her own pain. If she hasn't, she'll most likely choose Option #2. That is, she'll be furious with Denise. She'll run home, pick up the phone, and call Wendy. "You're not gonna believe what Denise just said to me. She does this stuff all the time. I can't stand her. When I hang up, I'm calling the pastor and telling him to forget about it: I'm resigning from the retreat committee."

To which Wendy responds, "That's nothing! You should hear what Denise said about Mildred. She said her grandson is a homosexual. I don't know if it's true, but you know he just moved to San Francisco. What does *that* tell you?"

Well, Sue doesn't know what to think of that, but she does know one thing. She's sick of being treated so unfairly at the First Christian Church. "I've had it with that church," she declares. "If that's the way people want to be, then I'll just go somewhere else. And they call themselves *Christians!*"

Kind of crazy, when you think about it. Sue has just allowed someone else's low opinion of her to become the centerpiece of her existence. Tell me you've never done the same thing!

The Heart of the Matter

Now we're getting to the heart of the matter. What determines which option Sue will choose? Quite simply this: whether or not she has allowed God to uproot her own destructive seeds. Let me change the scenario just slightly, and this will become obvious to you. Let's imagine these two women back at the restaurant. Denise turns to Sue and shouts, "Oh, no!!! You have pink giraffes growing out of your ears!!!"

Is this going to throw Sue for an emotional loop? Is she going to run home in an angry snit and start dialing for dollars? Is she going to storm the pastor's office and quit the church? No. She's going to recognize that this is not about her. It's about Denise. Denise has serious problems and needs serious prayer. When we see the other person's brokenness, it's so much easier to let go of our own hurt.

> " When we see the other person's brokenness, it's so much easier to let go of our own hurt. "

Sue will only react in anger and bitterness IF—now don't miss this part—IF Denise's words resonate with something deep inside of her. That is to say, if the destructive seed is still flourishing within her. The reason Sue flips out is because *the words ring true.* A familiar voice begins whispering in her ear: "She's right. You can't sing. You made a fool of yourself last year. You'll never be good enough. Don't ever try again." Depending on which game the enemy is playing, he might try the opposite approach: "Aha! They found you out. They all know what a phony you are! You better run. Better hide. Quick, go to another church and try harder next time."

Each lie is like a button in our heart. And every time one of those buttons gets pressed, we jump! And when we jump, we inevitably bump into other people, and when we do, someone is bound to get hurt. The more buttons you have, the more jumping you do. The more people you bump into, the more people you hurt. And since you're bumping and jumping all the time, you're hurt and exhausted in the process.

To be honest, I had so many buttons in my heart, all you had to say to me was "Donna, you look pretty today" and I'd get offended. I'd be thinking, *What? You thought I looked ugly yesterday?* Or "Donna, hey, you look like you've lost weight." My gut reaction would be *What? You thought I looked fat?* So no matter what anyone said, I took offense. I would always "take it the wrong way." Of course, if you said *nothing* about my personal appearance or weight-loss efforts, I'd get offended about that too. There was just no winning with me.

Release the Lie

Now do you see the power of those childhood lies? Do you see how they can have a profound impact on your current behavior? How they can shape even the most casual interactions in your everyday life? That's why it is so incredibly important to release the lie and neutralize the power of the past. As is often said, your history doesn't have to equal your destiny.

The lie the enemy planted in my heart was pretty basic: No one wants to play with you. No one ever will. Everyone you meet will reject you. Guaranteed. You might as well go ahead and give them a good reason to do it, so you can get it over with. It's the same basic lie he tells most kids: You're less than everyone else. You'll never measure up. You're not good enough, so don't even bother to try. Alternatively: You're not good enough, so you better try harder, try harder, try harder, try harder, until you drive yourself into a premature grave.

You didn't sign up to be lied to . . . but you were lied to anyway. The first step toward breaking free from the pain of your childhood is releasing the lie. Ask God, right now, to show you the lie that was planted. Then ask him to bring to your remembrance the very moment it was first planted and occasions when it was well watered. Fearlessly face the pain of those moments. Face the lie head on and see it for what it was and is: a device of the enemy.

Once you have done that, you are ready to ask the Holy Spirit to operate: to reach in and surgically remove the lie. Realize that he may need to do some "exploratory surgery" in the process, and in so doing he may reveal tumors and cancerous growths that you didn't even know you had. Rather than being frightened by that, be encouraged. God never reveals our pain just to hurt us. He reveals it so he can heal it. The fact that you didn't know about the disease doesn't mean it hasn't been silently killing you. If you are routinely angry, offended, or disappointed, I guarantee you've got a lie that needs to be uprooted.

At some point, no doubt while you are recovering from the

> *God never reveals our pain just to hurt us. He reveals it so he can heal it.*

surgery, you've got to have the following conversation with the Destructive Seed Planter.

I'm not going to believe your lies—not one more day. I refuse to let this defeat me. I've wasted enough years allowing the pain of my childhood to control me. The people who hurt me have no right to determine my destiny. They don't deserve that much power over my life. I'm not going to let them rent space in my head anymore. I am hereby serving them—and you—with eviction notices. Get out! And while I'm at it, I'm going to close the door on you by choosing to forgive the people who hurt me most. I know they inflicted pain because they were in pain.

Yearbook Reality Check

Not long ago I was visiting a friend's house when she broke out her high school yearbook and insisted I take a look. Truth be told, I had no desire to look at her yearbook. For me, high school was a painful place filled with intimidating characters—big, frightening giants. Imagine my surprise when I began leafing through the pages and saw a bunch of hapless teenagers. Gradually it occurred to me: *Her yearbook looks exactly like mine. This could be my high school. All the same cast of characters, the same cliques, even the same hairstyles and, no doubt, the same insecurities.*

It was one of those rare moments when I stopped being the only person in the world who had to endure life's little indignities. I felt a tenderness in my heart that embraced every teenager in America—

and every one of my fellow humans who had survived the journey and gone on to adulthood. As we realize that we're not alone, that everyone has a story to tell, it brings our own life into perspective.

Perspective is a beautiful thing.

I DIDN'T

~~Sign~~

UP FOR

DISAPPOINTING

RELATIONSHIPS

CHAPTER THREE

I Didn't Sign Up for Disappointing Relationships

In chapter 2 we discovered that just as God works through human vessels to accomplish his purposes on the earth, so does the enemy. As I've ministered to women around the country, it has become increasingly obvious that the area of greatest heartache is disappointing relationships. No one walks down the aisle thinking, *Gee, I hope this man makes me miserable for the rest of my life.* No one reaches out in friendship to another person thinking, *I'm looking forward to the day when this person totally betrays me.* No one signs up for disappointing relationships. But in the real world, we all have them. If we're honest, we also have the pain of knowing we have been a disappointment to others.

Forgiveness the Tool

Because we are all just jars of clay, it's inevitable that we will disappoint one another on a fairly routine basis. In fact, just last

Friday night I had to pull my twelve-year-old daughter aside and say, "Listen, I know you are disappointed in Mommy right now, and I'm so sad about that. I promise you I'm going to try harder. I hope you'll be able to forgive me." If you haven't had a similar conversation with one of your children recently, you're probably overdue.

I firmly believe the power to forgive is the most powerful tool—and the most precious gift—God has given us. I wonder why we don't use it more often? When we seek forgiveness, we make ourselves vulnerable. We acknowledge our frailty and ask for another chance. When we extend forgiveness, I believe we are closer to the heart of God than at any other time. Colossians 3:13 says, "Bear with each other and forgive whatever grievances you may have against one another. Forgive as the Lord forgave you."

> **"**
> *The more forgiving and gracious we are to others, the more people are willing to extend forgiveness and grace to us.*
> **"**

How did the Lord forgive us? Unconditionally. When did the Lord forgive us? When we least deserved it. I'm finding that the universe makes more and more sense as I apply the fundamental realization that nine times out of ten, we get what we give. This is even true in the area of forgiveness: "Forgive, and you will be forgiven" (Luke 6:37). The more forgiving and gracious we are to others, the more people are willing to extend forgiveness and grace to us. As we become increasingly willing to give others "the benefit of the doubt," others will do the same for us. Very few people are genuinely malicious or "out to get you." Those who are need a Savior, not our condemnation or anger. Look how Jesus responded to the people who crucified him: "Jesus said, 'Father, forgive them, for they do not know what they are doing'" (Luke 23:34).

He gave them the benefit of the doubt to the "nth" degree, wouldn't you say? As you spend time in prayer, seeking God's perspective on your disappointing relationships, God will give you the same revelation in a very personal way. Eventually you will come to that glorious place of freedom when you release the pain and cry out, "Father, forgive _____, for he did not know what he was doing."

Is There an *If* in Forgiveness?

God takes the matter of forgiveness very seriously: "For if you forgive men when they sin against you, your heavenly Father will also forgive you. But if you do not forgive men their sins, your Father will not forgive your sins" (Matthew 6:14–15).

I don't know about you, but I find the word *if* in the above verse rather frightening! In fact, my kids and I refer to this as "the scariest verse in the Bible." I find it difficult to reconcile this passage with the foundation of my theology, which says, "If you confess with your mouth, 'Jesus is Lord,' and believe in your heart that God raised him from the dead, you will be saved" (Romans 10:9). I mean, you pray the prayer and you're good to go, right? Still, the *if* remains and, frankly, I'm not sure what to do with it. Here's what I've told my daughters (if you have a better explanation, please e-mail me):

If we are unwilling to forgive others, then we haven't really understood what the Cross means. We haven't really understood the price Jesus paid for our sins—and how can we truly believe when we don't even understand? Consider the following passage from Matthew 18, the parable of the unforgiving debtor:

> Then Peter came to Jesus and asked, "Lord, how many times shall I forgive my brother when he sins against me? Up to seven times?"
>
> Jesus answered, "I tell you, not seven times, but seventy-seven times.
>
> "Therefore, the kingdom of heaven is like a king who wanted to settle accounts with his servants. As he began the settlement, a man who owed him ten thousand talents was brought to him. Since he was not able to pay, the master ordered that he and his wife and his children and all that he had be sold to repay the debt.
>
> "The servant fell on his knees before him. 'Be patient with me,' he begged, 'and I will pay back everything.' The servant's master took pity on him, canceled the debt and let him go.
>
> "But when that servant went out, he found one of his fellow servants who owed him a hundred denarii. He grabbed him and began to choke him. 'Pay back what you owe me!' he demanded.
>
> "His fellow servant fell to his knees and begged him, 'Be patient with me, and I will pay you back.'
>
> "But he refused. Instead, he went off and had the man thrown into prison until he could pay the debt. When the other servants saw what had happened, they were greatly distressed

and went and told their master everything that had happened.

"Then the master called the servant in. 'You wicked servant,' he said, 'I canceled all that debt of yours because you begged me to. Shouldn't you have had mercy on your fellow servant just as I had on you?' In anger his master turned him over to the jailers to be tortured, until he should pay back all he owed.

"This is how my heavenly Father will treat each of you unless you forgive your brother from your heart" (Matthew 18:21–35).

Unforgiveness and the Schemes of the Enemy

When we truly understand what God has done for us, forgiving others will become second nature. In the following passage, Paul is warning a local church against holding grudges, due to the destructive power of unforgiveness:

> If you forgive anyone, I also forgive him. And what I have forgiven—if there was anything to forgive—I have forgiven in the sight of Christ for your sake, in order that Satan might not outwit us. For we are not unaware of his schemes. (2 Corinthians 2:10–11)

You may be thinking, what does forgiveness have to do with Satan and his schemes? EVERYTHING! He knows the power of forgiveness better than anyone. It was God's willingness to provide a means of forgiveness for the human race that foiled Satan's plans at the Cross. What is Satan's scheme in your life? Real simple. To keep you stuck. To keep you so focused on who did what, and who said what, and how dare they, and you've had it, etc., that you can't move forward with the rest of your life. Trust me on this one. I know from personal experience.

I'll never forget meeting a woman at one of my conferences. She had tears in her eyes as she told me she had gone through a painful divorce. I reached out my hand to comfort her. Her whole body was trembling with hurt. Her words were filled with resentment; her tone of voice dripped with bitterness. I assumed the wound was fresh. However, as her story began to unfold, I realized this was not a recent occurrence. When I asked her how long ago she had gotten divorced, she replied, "Twenty-two years." I just about fell on the floor.

What a victory for the enemy. No wonder this woman's entire family lived in upheaval. No wonder her health was a wreck. She may not have signed up for a disappointing relationship; she certainly didn't sign up for divorce; but until she forgives her ex-husband, she is signing up DAILY to let the enemy have a field day with her life.

I want to come back to where we left off in the last chapter. Remember we asked the Holy Spirit to uproot the lie planted in your heart by the Destructive Seed Planter? We can't leave things there! Once you have asked the Holy Spirit to uproot the lie, it will probably be painfully obvious who Satan used to plant it there in the first place. You might also recognize a variety of seed-waterers who were used to reinforce the lie. The temptation is to let those revelations make you bitter. Although chances are you are already filled with bitterness toward them, even if it's only on a subconscious level. As a little aside: Do you have a person in your life to whom you invariably speak in a certain "tone of voice"? Even when they haven't done anything offensive at that particular moment? That's your cue to look for deep-seated bitterness that needs to be dealt with.

You should take these revelations as your invitation to forgive the person or people involved. Realize they were just pawns in a cruel game. In their own way, they were most certainly victims before they became victimizers.

Overcoming Resentment

My daughter Leah had been hurt—devastated, actually—by the behavior of someone she loved very much. As a result, I could see that a root of bitterness and resentment was beginning to grow. Hebrews 12:15 warns us: "See to it that no one misses the grace of God and that no bitter root grows up to cause trouble and defile many." Bitterness is like a contagious disease: first it spreads throughout our own body; then it begins to overtake the people around us.

One night as we sat talking, God led me to share with her a quote from Henri Nouwen:

> **"**
>
> *Bitterness is like a contagious disease: first it spreads throughout our own body; then it begins to overtake the people around us.*
>
> **"**

One way for me to deal with my resentment is to acknowledge the suffering of the other person. Whenever I'm hurt, I perceive the other person as strong, and myself as weak. But when I'm willing to consider the other person's individual history with struggle and agony, I can prevent myself from judging too harshly or making a final angry statement about their behavior.[1]

Rather than focusing on how this person had disappointed her and the pain this person had inflicted (and isn't it always a temptation to retell and rehash old hurts?), we talked about the pain the person had endured. It didn't excuse her actions, but it did explain them. An article I read recently put it this way:

> Significant acts of forgiveness entail letting go of a precious story we tell about ourselves, risking the awareness of a larger, less self-justifying truth. . . . Owning up means getting past one's defensiveness. It means stepping out of the Blaming System, in which one person has to be not only wrong but also the bad one.[2]

Agonizing Forgiveness

One danger with forgiveness, which is prevalent in the church, is something I would call "rushed forgiveness" or "sweep-it-under-

---

[1]Henri Nouwen, *From Fear to Love: Lenten Reflections on the Parable of the Prodigal Son,* 15.
[2]Robert Karen, *O* magazine, February 2001.

the-carpet" forgiveness. Sometimes well-meaning people who don't want to face life's more painful realities want to use forgiveness like a magic wand. They think it can make all the pain disappear and wipe out logical consequences.

My friend Martha faced this when she went through a personal crisis several years ago. She discovered that her husband had been conducting a five-year affair with a teenage girl. She vividly remembers trying to tell her pastor what was going on, but he literally put his hand up and said, "I don't need to hear intimate details." He didn't want to face it. It was too horrible, so he wanted her to sweep it under the carpet. His remedy was "Just forgive and forget about the whole thing" with the subtext being "I really don't want to face the truth that families who sit in my congregation with smiles on their faces could be living through the hell you are about to describe. If I allow myself to hear this, I will lose my plausible deniability. You'll rob me of the right to pretend this stuff can't possibly happen in Christian homes. And I don't think I can survive that. So please shut up and go away. You're scaring me."

That's not forgiveness; that's denial.

There can be no authentic forgiveness as long as we are in denial. I think it's extremely significant that the parable of the unforgiving debtor lists EXACTLY what the debt owed was, down to a fraction of a penny. That is so key! Until we confront the true cost, until we come face to face with what has been stolen from us and how we have been forced to pay a heavy price for the sins of others, I don't think there can be true forgiveness. When Jesus pondered the Cross—when he considered paying the price for our sins—he carefully counted the cost. Indeed, the Scripture tells us: "And being in anguish, he prayed more earnestly, and his sweat was like drops of blood falling to the ground" (Luke 22:44).

That's what I call agonizing forgiveness. It doesn't run and hide. It doesn't bury an offense or pretend it didn't matter. It looks the pain straight in the eye and says, "You hurt me so bad you nearly killed me, but because Christ died for me, his love compels me to forgive you." Nothing short of *that* type of forgiveness will ever change your life.

A Higher Court

You can sweep sin under the carpet in an instant, but I believe "agonizing forgiveness" often requires a process and it may unfold over the course of time. The only One who was capable of forgiving once for all was Jesus. The rest of us have to work on it every stinkin' day. For me personally, forgiving the one who hurt me most has been a long, slow journey. Just when I think I've finished the work, the Lord will show me something else I need to deal with. Now, what I'm about to share doesn't mean we should endlessly rehash old wounds and hurts. However, we do have to face facts. At one point, God actually led me to make a list detailing exactly what this person's sin had cost me. It brought me as close to "sweating drops of blood" as I have ever come in my entire life. I

> "*Agonizing forgiveness*" *often requires a process and it may unfold over the course of time.*

cried day and night for weeks. At one point, my daughter asked me if I thought I would ever stop crying. I told her I didn't know for sure. And I honestly didn't.

God forced me to confront the full truth. And just when the pain was about to overwhelm me, God said, "Now give me the list." I felt like the Lord gave me a word picture at that time. I was sitting in a courtroom with my list. I was the plaintiff, the prosecuting attorney, and the judge all rolled into one. I was forcefully presenting my case and passing judgments left and right. The Lord stepped into the courtroom and said, "As long as you are still trying this case—as long as it's tied up in the lower court—it will never pass to a Higher Court."

Instantly I understood. I needed to let go of this person so God could deal with him. *Perfect,* I thought to myself, *God can dish out the punishment his sins deserve and will do a much better job of it than I can.* For a moment I was overjoyed. But then I heard God say, "What if my judgment is to grant him the same forgiveness you were granted at the foot of the cross?"

"No, Lord!" I cried. "No. Please. Don't! I want you to punish him. I want you to vindicate me before the whole world by publicly condemning him. I want you to *make him pay* for what he's done to me."

"Then you haven't really forgiven him, have you?" came the reply.

Apparently not.

I'm still working on it.

No doubt significant people in your life have disappointed

you . . . some in small ways, others profoundly so. You didn't sign up for disappointing relationships, but they signed up for you. Now the question remains: What will you do? Will you live your life consumed by the bitterness? Will you sweep the pain under the carpet? Or will you work through the process of "agonizing forgiveness" until you finally reach that place where you entrust yourself entirely to him who judges justly? (1 Peter 2:23). If you are willing to cooperate with God, he is able to heal the hurt and, in so doing, you'll be well on your way to discovering the life you signed up for. A life where old hurts are left behind to make room for new joys.

I DIDN'T

×*Sign*

UP TO MAKE

FOOLISH CHOICES

I Didn't Sign Up to Make Foolish Choices

My house was absolutely freezing. One night it was so cold in my bedroom, my body hurt from shivering. I kept putting more pellets into our wood-burning stove and turning it higher and higher. I even turned up the electric heater, which I normally only use as a backup system. But no matter how high I turned the pellet stove, no matter how high I turned the electric thermostat, it was still freezing in the house, especially upstairs. I thought, *There must be something wrong with the ventilation system.* I went throughout the house, carefully checking each of the heat vents to make sure they were, indeed, spitting out hot air. All seemed to be in good working order.

Maybe I need to have the pellet stove cleaned out; maybe it's clogged or something, I thought. So I had someone come and clean out the pellet stove.

I need to add insulation to the windows, I thought. I'd seen those ads on TV where you put up this plastic Saran Wrap–type stuff, then blow-dry it. *Yeah, something like that might do the trick.*

I was wracking my little brain trying to come up with solutions, but nothing seemed to work. I was completely baffled. This went on for several days. Finally, I identified the coldest room. Then honed in on the coldest location. I lifted up the blinds and *voila!* An open window.

Boy, did I let out a scream!

"TAAAAAAAAAAAAAARRRRRRRRRRRAAAAAAAAAAA!"

That's Tara, by the way. As in my five-year-old. She came running into the room. I had now gathered my wits about me. "You wouldn't happen to know anything about this open window, would you?"

She knew she was in big trouble. "I wanted to watch the worker man," she said sheepishly. Let me tell you, that little girl got the lecture of a lifetime about opening windows in winter, electric bills, money not growing on trees, ingratitude, etc., etc., etc.

A couple of weeks later, I noticed that my house was really cold again. *Well, the weather is intensifying. We're on the side of a mountain; it's like a giant wind tunnel. Four walls can only keep the cold out to some degree. Better turn up that pellet stove. Boy, I'm needing to rely on that back-up electric heater a lot more than I did last year.*

Do I scare you?

Anyway, this whole *Wow, it's so much colder than last year* internal monologue went on for a couple of days until I finally had an epiphany: *Donna, why don't you check Tara's window?*

DUH.

Guess what? Tara had opened another window!

Now, I'm not saying it was God's idea for Tara to disobey me after I had given her such clear directives against opening windows.

But let me tell you, God sure used it to get my attention. And I do believe he sent me the message twice because he was determined I not miss it.

So what's the message? Here goes.

I had known for many years that there was something seriously wrong in my spiritual life. There were significant areas of sin that seemed absolutely entrenched, unconquerable. No matter how hard I tried to "turn up the heat" through attending a weekly women's Bible study and having a personal devotional time, I could not seem to move forward. Even days spent in prayer and fasting left me feeling "out in the cold."

I kept thinking there must be something wrong with the "heating system." Or that I needed to turn the heat higher and higher with more prayer, more Bible reading, and more study. Through Tara and the open windows, God showed me—in a very vivid way—that even though there was nothing wrong with my heating system, I could still be left out in the cold if I didn't do something about the open windows in my life. Those open windows were my judgmental attitude and my unwillingness to forgive those who had hurt me.

Baffling Array of Tests

Throughout my Christian life, I've always been baffled by the fact that I seem to face a lot more tests than other people. I thought God was picking on me. Or that the universe was just this terribly unjust, confusing place. Or, alternatively, I flattered myself that God was "allowing" all these tests because:

- I was a spiritual giant and He knew I could handle them all.
- He was using all of these experiences to mold my character so that I could be a shining beacon of godliness in a lost world.
- I was a spiritual giant so Satan was unfairly targeting me for attack.

Sometimes God does allow "the testing of our faith," as it says in James 1:2–4:

> Consider it pure joy, my brothers, whenever you face trials of many kinds, because you know that the testing of your faith develops perseverance. Perseverance must finish its work so that you may be mature and complete, not lacking anything.

But when I looked at my own life, I had to conclude that something else was going on. The fact of the matter was, I was not a spiritual giant. I was a wreck. These experiences were not molding my character; they were warping my character. I'll say more about the fairness or unfairness of the enemy's attacks in the next chapter. I think we've got enough to deal with already.

So Many Judgments

One day God gave me a little revelation. "The reason you have so many tests is because you pass so many judgments!" I began pondering this idea. I should probably confess that I used to be one of those delightful people who knew exactly what was wrong with everyone and everything. You see, I had the precious "gift of discernment." I would spend hours, literally, delivering silent sermons to everyone who had done me wrong. I pronounced judgments like a soda machine spits out cans: routinely, easily, and thoughtlessly. Yet the Scripture specifically states: "Do not judge, or you too will be judged. For in the same way you judge others, you will be judged, and with the measure you use, it will be measured to you" (Matthew 7:1–2).

God has set up the spiritual realm in such a way that you get what you give. It's called reaping what you sow, and it's one of the most powerful realities in the universe. I wasn't getting what God wanted to give me; I was just getting back what I was giving the world. So while it was true enough

> *God is never glad for our sin or its consequences.*

that a sovereign God "allowed" me to reap the logical consequences of my sin, that's a completely different mindset than "God is allowing this trial" as in it was his idea somehow. God is never glad for our sin or its consequences. He specifically commands us, "Do NOT" do these things. And he warns us in advance what will happen when we violate these fundamental principles of the universe.

Does God Really Mean That?

I had always dismissed these verses, just like I conveniently dismissed any other verse that didn't fit in with my existing theology or mindset. I can actually remember explaining them away like so: "Well, this can't mean what it looks like it means. Because I know

Jesus already forgave all my sin, so I am not under judgment. This must apply to all those terrible non-Christians who pick on me at work just because I'm a self-consumed, insecure lunatic. But hey, I'm forgiven and they're not. So ha-ha! Oops. Gotta hurry up and get to Bible study now. Too bad Kathy never shuts up. Bob is leading tonight. He is so clueless. The group would be waaay better if they let me lead it. I guess they're just jealous of my superior biblical insight."

Gee, sorta makes you want to come play with me, huh?

I got an early jump on judging the world. It started with my family. Unfortunately, I thought I was so much better than all of them, I could hardly stand living in the same house. Clearly, I had been switched at birth. I blamed my brothers and my sister for ruining my life. They weren't the siblings I signed up for. I signed up for the Brady Bunch. For Greg and Marsha, whose worst crisis was a pimple on their forehead. I signed up for family problems that could be resolved in thirty minutes—less time out for commercials. My siblings didn't measure up, so I judged them. That was my first seriously bad move.

I didn't understand what I understand now. When we judge another human being, we set in motion some powerful spiritual forces. It's like whistling for the devil. It's like inviting him to bring on the test: to tempt us with the same stuff we judged another person for being unable to withstand. I was a freshman in high school when the enemy showed up and said, "So, you'd never be a drug addict like your brothers and sister? You're better than they are, huh? Let's just see about that."

I took the test and flunked. I never signed up to become a drug addict . . . but I became one anyway.

Perhaps the group I judged most harshly were divorced Christians. What a disgrace to the cause of Christ! They should be ashamed of themselves, tearing their children apart and single-handedly destroying the fabric of American society. How dare they show their faces in church ever again? I mean, how superficial can you be? Okay, so your husband had a little affair. Big deal. Get over it! I mean, you didn't see ME getting divorced and I can personally guarantee that my marriage was ten times worse than all other bad marriages in the history of unholy matrimony combined.

I think you know where *that* took me.

But I didn't "get it" back then, so I was blindsided when the test came. When my marriage ended in divorce, all the judgments I had passed came raining down on my head. Then I experienced first-hand the excruciating pain of rejection and condemnation of fellow believers. But God is a redeemer. And it was this very experience that God finally used to get through to my thick skull. "Donna, you want to scream from the highest mountain, 'You don't know what he's done to me! You have no idea what I've lived through.' That's exactly how all the women you judged felt. You have no idea why people do half the things they do. And it's none of your business anyway. It's my business. Your business is to love people unconditionally. You have no other assignment."

Back to the Beginning

So what does all this have to do with making foolish choices? Bear with me for another paragraph or so. We're getting there. You see, I wish I had known these truths as a new believer. My Christian walk would have been an entirely different experience. Let me take you back to the beginning and you can witness firsthand where I went wrong.

My life took a dramatic turn for the better when a friend invited me to take a free vacation in the mountains of northern Pennsylvania. Nothing could have fully prepared me for my trip to Tuscarora, a Lutheran Brethren Retreat Center. Actually, a group of Presbyterians were hosting the event I attended and I often joke that "nothing in the Westminster Shorter Catechism could have prepared them for the likes of me!" Somewhere around the third day, I was sitting along the Delaware River, when suddenly I understood: God had made a way for me to get a second chance at life. When Jesus came to earth 2,000 years ago, he came so that we could have life. He died so that we could live. He took the punishment we deserved so that we wouldn't have to face it on our own. God was offering me a free gift; all I had to do was accept it. So I accepted it with all my heart.

And let me tell you, the day I signed up to follow Jesus . . . I signed up to change the world. In fact, the night after I became a Christian, I was walking alone under a beautiful moonlit sky when I heard God speak to me so clearly it was as if he were walking beside me. He said, "Donna, I'm going to take you to retreat centers just like this one all over the country, and I'm going to use you in a mighty way in my kingdom."

I couldn't believe it! The God of the universe had *picked me*. I had always felt like the last person anyone would ever pick. Maybe you were like me: you can remember dreading P. E. class and the whole "dividing into teams" drill. I was almost always one of the last kids picked. It went something like this:

"We're not gonna take her; you take her."

"No, we're not gonna take her."

"Tell you what. We'll give you Donna and a ten-point lead."

"Forget it."

"We'll give you Donna, a ten-point lead, and the new aluminum bat."

I know what it feels like to be the "unpicked one." Maybe you do, too. So I was thrilled beyond belief to know that the God of the universe had picked me. John 15:16 says, "You did not choose me, but I chose you. . . . *to sit in the pew and take notes concerning what's wrong with everyone at your church.*" Being a zealous new believer, I set right to work on the assignment. I only recently discovered that I had misread the verse. Actually, it says, "You did not choose me, but I chose you and appointed you to go and bear fruit—fruit that will last. Then the Father will give you whatever you ask in my name."

It gets even worse. The *very next* verse reads, "This is my command: Love each other" (John 15:17).

How I Blew It Big-Time

Well, back in the beginning—you know, back when I knew so much—I wasn't real concerned about loving people. I was out to change the world, unlike the lightweight, superficial Christians surrounding me. I'd been a Christian for a few weeks, so I think I had a better grasp on Christianity than *they* did. I had waited a long time to get picked for something and I wasn't gonna blow it. Except I *did* blow it.

Many of you already know my testimony, but for those who don't, I'll recap briefly. Shortly after becoming a Christian, I went off to college. The very first week, I met a young Middle Eastern Muslim man who dramatically changed the course of my life. Although I knew God specifically said, "Do not be yoked together with unbelievers" (2 Corinthians 6:14), I chose to become entangled with him anyway. Even though everyone around me pointed out my disobedience, I had started down the path and couldn't find a way to turn back. We married in 1982, and for the next eighteen years he exerted an extraordinary degree of control over my life. Even though he converted to Christianity, his cultural roots ran deep. As is customary in many Middle Eastern countries, I was not permitted to leave the house without his permission and strict supervision. To him, this was perfectly logical. He was "protecting" me because he loved me so much. Why would any decent woman want to go somewhere without her husband? What was I trying to hide? If I wasn't planning to do anything wrong, why should I object to his keeping constant watch over my every move?

It was absolutely maddening . . . but my husband couldn't figure out why I was going nuts. I remember one day in particular, I wanted to go for a walk around the block by myself—something I had always been strictly forbidden to do. So I asked my husband's permission, but the answer was "No." I asked, "Can I at least sit on the front steps?" The answer was "No." As you can imagine, it's pretty tough to travel to retreat centers around the country when you're not allowed to sit on the front steps.

I didn't sign up to make foolish choices, but I had made a colossal one. So often we want to blame God for our predicament. Or we offer the excuse, "Well, God is in control, so it must be God's will." No, it is never God's will for us to be disobedient.

> *It is never God's will for us to be disobedient.*

My life was NOT where God wanted it to be; it was where my own foolish choices had brought me.

Is it possible you need to make some painful admissions about your own life?

Irrevocable Mistakes?

If my story ended there, this would be a seriously depressing book. Praise God, he is moving me forward to find hope and healing. I was so afraid my mistakes were irreversible. But God reassured me from his Word: "God's gifts and his call are irrevocable" (Romans 11:29). God is bigger than our mistakes.

But. Here's the big but. But, at some point, we have to truly repent. We have to stop blaming God and agree with God. We have to turn around and change directions. That's what real repentance means. It's not enough to feel sorry. We have to change the way we're living.

"This isn't the life I signed up for," but when I'm completely honest, it's pretty much the logical outcome of my life choices . . . and the choices of those around me. That's not always the case. Sometimes life throws people a genuine curve ball. Something absolutely out of our control, like a child born with birth defects. I'll say more about that later, but this is the chapter on foolish mistakes. I know for me personally, there weren't any curve balls. Just my own stupidity.

Return to Tuscarora

Before I tell the next story, I have to preface it with one important piece of background information: I was born in a small town in southern New Jersey, situated along the Delaware River. Okay, keep that in mind, and here we go.

I was invited to return to Tuscarora in November 2001 as the featured speaker for two back-to-back women's retreats. For months I eagerly anticipated the trip. I prayed and asked God to meet me there, once more, just as powerfully and personally as he did the first time. I arrived late at night and was shown to my room overlooking the Delaware River. In the morning, I joyously walked down to the river's edge, hoping to hear from God. But when I looked at the river, my spirit was suddenly in turmoil. I could tell by the leaves on the surface that the water was churning in circles and seemed to be going nowhere. I looked more closely and it appeared to be flowing south to north. *This is madness,* I thought. *I was born on this river. I KNOW it flows north to south!*

I can't describe what happened to me next, other than to say it felt like a panic attack. I literally ran back to my cabin and hid under the covers all day. (The conference didn't start until that evening.) Throughout my first few days at the conference, whenever I wasn't speaking or eating, I was often hiding under the covers. I couldn't understand what was happening to me. I couldn't believe how lethargic I felt. I kept saying to myself, *Snap out of it, girl. This is a momentous occasion. You should be communing with God. You should be on the spiritual high of your life. What's wrong with you?*

One day I went and sat on a bench and prayed, "God, speak to me! I need to hear from you!" and a still, small voice within me said, "You first." I began pouring out my heart to God. I knelt down in the dirt and wept before him, laying down every disappointment, every stupid choice, every broken piece of my shattered life. I laid down everything I had tried to do but had failed at. I laid down my failed marriage. I laid down my troubled children. I laid down my fledgling ministry. I laid it all down and surveyed the ruins, weeping uncontrollably.

Then God brought to my remembrance a scene from my favorite movie, *Out of Africa*. It recounts the true story of Karen Blixen, an author who moved from Denmark to Kenya, hoping to build a better life. Instead, she experienced one catastrophe after another— none of which she signed up for. Her husband made a series of foolish financial decisions, then abandoned her. Her farm was nearly wiped out by a flood. She recovered, only to have it destroyed by fire.

She began her journey to Africa with high hopes and fine china. She served as benefactress to the local village, providing them with employment and health care. The children had become accustomed to finding little treats in her pockets. But eventually all was stripped away. In the movie, as she watched her farm burn to the ground, a little child runs up and reaches into her pocket, but there's nothing there. Karen Blixen stares off into the distance and mumbles softly, "All gone. All gone."

As I knelt in the dirt that day, I mumbled the same words: "All gone. All gone, Father." Gone is all the good advice I thought I could give people. Gone the urge to tell anyone else how to live. Gone every word I felt qualified to speak. Gone the need to build a name for myself. All gone. All gone. I prayed, "Lord, everything I thought I had to offer this world is gone. From now on the only thing I'll give is whatever you give me."

Two days before the conference ended, I walked down to the river again. But this time it was completely different. The current was strong and the river was clearly flowing north to south. "Yes! I knew it!" I wanted to shout! I was so filled with joy, I ran three miles on the scenic road that curves alongside the river, and it felt like a walk around the block.[1] I was completely energized as I took in the beauty of my surroundings: the fall colors everywhere, the sound of leaves crushing under my feet.

Suddenly Hebrews 12:1–2 came to mind, but the Lord personalized it for me: "Therefore since you are surrounded by such a great cloud of witnesses, you need to throw off everything that hinders

---

[1] I should probably mention that I was training for a 5K at the time, so I was certainly capable of running three miles. I had just been too lethargic to do it.

and the sin that so easily entangles, so you can run with perseverance the race I've marked out for you. Fix your eyes on Jesus, the
author and perfecter of your faith."

Later that day God opened my eyes to see the meaning behind
my two trips to the river. The first trip symbolized my first visit to
Tuscarora in 1980. Even though I knew which direction God had
told me to go, I chose to go the opposite way, and it threw my life
into turmoil. My life was going nowhere. The lethargy symbolized
the coping mechanism I used to survive the pain of my marriage. I
vividly remember waking up many mornings and just saying, "No.
This can't be happening. This can't be my life." Then I'd roll over
and try to sleep some more. I was chronically depressed, which low-
ered my body's immune system and made me chronically sick and
barely able to function.

Another thing the Lord showed me was that it would not have
upset me to observe the river flowing south to north if I didn't know
any better. But since I had been born on that river, I knew in my
heart something was wrong. Many people can walk in disobedience
to God and not experience inner turmoil. They spend their whole
lives blissfully flowing toward hell. But since I had been "born
again" along that river, I knew better.

The second trip to the river symbolized my second visit to Tuscarora. This time I not only knew which direction to go, I had the
courage and supernatural energy to "run with it." And to run with
great joy and perseverance. This was God's way of reassuring me
that I was now back on track, flowing in the direction he had
intended from the beginning.

I had wanted God to speak to me under the moonlight, just as he had during my first trip. So I had stood alone outside on several evenings. Not a peep from God. But on the last night of the conference, as I delivered my talk, God laid it on my heart to invite the ladies to join me down by the river, under the moonlight. I extended the invitation to any who might wish to come to meet me at 11:00 P.M. As the moment approached, I wondered if anyone would show up. The enemy was trying to fill my head with the same old lie: "Nobody wants to play with you. These women don't really like you." Approximately seventy-five women gathered together, praying and singing with me along the Delaware River, under the moonlight, until shortly after midnight. It was one of the most beautiful evenings of my life.[2]

As I walked slowly back to my cabin, the Lord gave me the final piece of the puzzle. "The reason you were unable to fulfill my call upon your life the first time is because you stood before me all alone. Now you are surrounded by a great crowd of witnesses— women all around the world who believe in you, pray for you, and want to cheer you on. This time you will run with perseverance the race I've set before you."

To Obey Is Better Than Sacrifice

Another thing God showed me at the river was this: You can't force a river to flow south to north, when it was created to flow

---

[2]Special thanks to Becky Braisted, Debbie Fawcett, and the wonderful Lutheran Brethren ladies who were part of this life-changing event. I will never forget you, my dear sisters!

north to south. The result will be turmoil.

No matter how hard I tried, I could not turn disobedience into obedience. My relationship with my former husband was an act of disobedience from the beginning, but I sincerely thought that if I sacrificed long enough and claimed to be "suffering for Jesus" (as opposed to "suffering for my own stupidity") that I could somehow make it look like obedience. It didn't work.

Am I saying that everyone who deliberately married outside the will of God
should rush out and get a divorce as an act
of obedience to God? Certainly not. God
can and does perform marriage miracles on
a daily basis. Stories abound of marriages
on the brink of ruin yet rescued in response
to the faith-filled prayers of one or both
partners. There are many couples who had

> *No matter how hard I tried, I could not turn disobedience into obedience.*

nothing in common, and no human chance to succeed, yet they are thriving, thanks to the grace and mercy of God.

I am not referring to such couples. I am referring to the basket cases, and I am saying, let's not spiritualize our predicament. Let's stop pretending we are "suffering for Jesus," when we are simply suffering for our own foolish choices. Let's not claim that God has "allowed this" as a means to "build our character" or he has placed us there "as a witness." That's exactly the type of thing I used to claim, but I was deceiving myself. God never promotes disobedience, and he never places his children in spiritually compromising positions. We do that on our own. This principle can be applied to

every area of our lives, from friendships to finances.

Saul tried to play this little game with God and it didn't work for him, either:

> Samuel said to Saul, "I am the one the Lord sent to anoint you king over his people Israel; so listen now to the message from the Lord. This is what the Lord Almighty says: 'I will punish the Amalekites for what they did to Israel when they waylaid them as they came up from Egypt. Now go, attack the Amalekites and totally destroy everything that belongs to them. Do not spare them; put to death men and women, children and infants, cattle and sheep, camels and donkeys.'"
>
> Then Saul attacked the Amalekites all the way from Havilah to Shur, to the east of Egypt. He took Agag king of the Amalekites alive, and all his people he totally destroyed with the sword. But Saul and the army spared Agag and the best of the sheep and cattle, the fat calves and lambs—everything that was good. These they were unwilling to destroy completely, but everything that was despised and weak they totally destroyed.
>
> Then the word of the Lord came to Samuel: "I am grieved that I have made Saul king, because he has turned away from me and has not carried out my instructions." Samuel was troubled, and he cried out to the Lord all that night.
>
> Early in the morning Samuel got up and went to meet Saul, but he was told, "Saul has gone to Carmel. There he has set up a monument in his own honor and has turned and gone on down to Gilgal."
>
> When Samuel reached him, Saul said, "The Lord bless you! I have carried out the Lord's instructions."

But Samuel said, "What then is this bleating of sheep in my ears? What is this lowing of cattle that I hear?"

Saul answered, "The soldiers brought them from the Amalekites; they spared the best of the sheep and cattle to sacrifice to the Lord your God, but we totally destroyed the rest" (1 Samuel 15:1–3, 7–15).

Wow, what a passage. God tells Saul exactly what to do, but Saul has a better idea. Sound familiar? God says, "Kill them all," but that seems so cruel and wasteful. Wouldn't it be better to spare some of those animals? I mean, wouldn't that just be better stewardship? Isn't God lucky to have us around, since we know so much more than he does?

I especially love verse 13, where Saul eagerly declares, "I did it for God." Yikes! Sounds like the old Donna! Maybe I'm getting a little cynical in my old age, but I'm at the place now where the more loudly someone insists they're "doing it for God" the higher I raise my eyebrows. The next verse is one of my favorite lines in the entire Bible—I mean, it's just absolutely hilarious when you think about it. Saul insists that he has obeyed God, but Samuel counters, "What then is this bleating of sheep in my ears?"

If Saul had obeyed God—and destroyed everything—he would not be surrounded by sheep, that's for sure.

Saul's circumstances contradict his claim!

Do your circumstances contradict your claims?

Now I'm really making you nervous, huh? Relax! I'm not saying your circumstances are the only measure of your obedience. I'm just asking you a simple question: Is your life filled with the bleating of sheep? That is, the negative logical consequences of your choices (or the choices of those closest to you). Saul chose to let the sheep live; that's why they were bleating. Maybe you chose to let your kids run wild, never taking time out of your hectic schedule to discipline them properly. Now they are living in rebellion. Or maybe you never let them think an independent thought, and *that's* why they're rebelling. Then again, maybe they're just making foolish choices because people routinely make foolish choices and your kids are no exception.

Spiritualizing Our Disobedience

Saul tried to spiritualize his disobedience. Now that he was surrounded by bleating sheep (that is, the circumstances created by his disobedience), he would offer it as a sacrifice to God. He honestly thought that somehow that would make it okay in God's eyes. He figured God would be so pleased with his *sacrifice*, he would overlook the *disobedience*. But that is not what God's Word says! Samuel tells Saul, in verse 22, "To obey is better than sacrifice." More than anything we can give God, be for God, do for God, he simply wants our heart. I very often find that when I have to work too hard at something, it's not from God. Whether it's a friendship I'm trying to "work at" or a ministry opportunity I'm trying to "work at," God's call is to simple obedience. As we obey him,

> " *More than anything we can give God, be for God, do for God, he simply wants our heart.* "

he sends the right people and opportunities our way without undue effort on our part. It shouldn't have to be forced.

Overturned Trash Can

If you're like me and you find yourself surrounded by a rather large herd of bleating sheep, you might be feeling discouraged right about now. So let me turn the corner and cheer you up with a little story about my new dog, Bea. Bea is a German shepherd guard dog. And when I say German, I mean she still sleeps in the kennel with the German airline flight sticker on the top. She is ostensibly one of the smartest dogs in the whole world—carefully bred, highly trained, able to do everything except load the dinner dishes into the dishwasher.

Well, Bea was not quite as smart as I had hoped nor as highly trained. (I love her anyway, of course!) One Saturday morning I woke up early and decided to make Bea a delicious treat of home-cooked chicken and rice. The reason I have to prepare home-cooked meals for the dog is because twenty years ago I judged my sister-in-law for preparing home-cooked meals for *her* German shepherd. And God never lets me get away with *anything!* I walked into the kitchen and discovered that Bea—one of the smartest, most well-trained dogs in the world, so clever she had to be imported directly from Germany—had snuck into the kitchen the night before and ripped apart the trash bag like some ordinary American mutt.

I brought her into the kitchen and firmly said, "Bad dog!" in

German (probably with a really bad German accent, but she got the message anyway). I was so furious with her! She tucked her tail under in disgrace and skulked away to her kennel (the one with the German airline sticker, which we leave on as a daily reminder of just how smart this dog is). I locked her in there so she could ponder her crime for a season.[3]

Well, now I was in a quandary. I fully intended to make Bea a special treat. She had been eating ordinary dog food for several days, and that's expecting a lot, considering what an extraordinary dog she is. So out came the rice cooker and the casserole dish at 7:00 A.M. on a weekend. (If you know anything about me, you know this is a remarkable turn of events.)

About forty-five minutes had transpired. When everything was ready, I opened the kennel door and encouraged Bea to "come and get it" with my best German accent. She wouldn't come. "You're gonna love it," I promised sweetly. She still wouldn't come. Now I was getting frustrated, because the food I had worked so hard to prepare was just sitting there.

I literally had to drag her out of the kennel and over to the food, which she normally devours. She hung her head and refused to eat. I sat down beside her and began hand-feeding her little pieces of warm chicken, all the while reassuring her that I still considered her a good dog. Eventually she got the idea and enjoyed the rest of the meal.

---

[3]The dog trainer has since told me my disciplinary technique was incorrect, so if you're a dog lover, rest easy about it.

You see, I was ready to restore our relationship. The fact that she had made a bad choice in no way changed my love for her. True, I had to discipline her. True, I had to allow her to suffer the logical consequences for a season (being confined to her kennel). But I didn't want her locked in there forever; she wasn't eternally doomed. I still wanted her to enjoy good gifts. Unfortunately, she wanted to prolong her punishment beyond what was required.

I have so much in common with animals, sometimes it scares me.

Forgiving Ourselves

Just because you've made foolish choices doesn't mean you're a bad person. Or that God hates you and you are doomed to a life of misery. God loves you and he gives second chances. People can learn from their mistakes and become better as a result.

Unfortunately, some people get stuck in a vicious cycle once they've made that first misstep. "When we feel worthless, we act worthless. Instead of faith ruling our lives, insecurity rules our thoughts and actions. We perceive ourselves a certain way, then we act out those perceptions."[4]

> *You are not the sum of your choices. You are who God says you are.*

It's like Bea. Suddenly she saw herself as a junkyard dog and conducted herself accordingly, cowering in her kennel like an

---

[4]Debbie Alsdorf, *Steadfast Love* (Cook Communications, 2000), 56.

| *THIS ISN'T THE LIFE I SIGNED UP FOR* |

enemy of the people. She momentarily forgot that she's an imported wonder-dog, worthy of home-cooked meals. You are *not* the sum of your choices. You are who God says you are:

> But you are a chosen people, a royal priesthood, a holy nation, a people belonging to God, that you may declare the praises of him who called you out of darkness into his wonderful light. Once you were not a people, but now you are the people of God; once you had not received mercy, but now you have received mercy. (1 Peter 2:9–10)

Okay, so you've made some foolish choices. Staying in the kennel with your head hung in shame and your tail tucked between your legs will get you nowhere. God forgives you; he still loves you. Come, enjoy the feast.

You've Gone Far Enough in That Way

Following is the first of several excerpts I want to share with you from a delightful devotional called *Come Away, My Beloved*.[5] Next to my Bible and prayer journal, it is currently my most treasured possession. I have written in the margin of my book, "11/12/01—Nailed me." Read on and see if it nails you too:

> You have made an arduous journey. You have climbed many
> a mountain that you could easily have walked around. You have

---

[5]I am taking the liberty of updating the language. The original text uses "thee" and "thy," etc.

often misconstrued My will and felt that only in sacrifice and suffering could you please Me, while much of the time I have longed to deliver you out of the very pains you thus inflicted upon yourself. You meant to please Me but in truth you were only marring your own beauty—which is precious to me.

I cannot rejoice in a blighted rose. You have gone far enough in that way. I offer you My path now, if you are strong enough to accept it. Life and liberty and love and joy. Health and peace—simplicity and rest. It has been there for you all along. You can have it even now if you will.[6]

Ah! Life. Liberty. Love. Joy. Health. Peace. Simplicity. Rest. Now, doesn't THAT sound like the life you signed up for?

---

[6]Frances J. Roberts, *Come Away, My Beloved* (Ojai, Calif.: King's Farspan, Inc., 1973), excerpts from 151–52. A new hardcover gift edition with language updates is now available from Barbour & Company (2002).

I DIDN'T

Sign

UP FOR

DISAPPOINTMENT

WITH GOD

CHAPTER FIVE

I Didn't Sign Up for Disappointment With God

Okay, here's a bold confession for you. I have rarely been disappointed with God, because I have tried my best never to *risk* disappointment with God. See if you can follow me on this. Everyone and everything in my life felt like such a disappointment, I feared that if I asked God for something and he didn't come through, I would totally fall apart. So I played the game of "low expectations." (Quick question: Does that sound like faith . . . or fear?)

Everything We Need?

One of my favorite passages is 2 Peter 1:3–9. However, I never fully understood what it actually meant until about half an hour ago as I was standing in the shower letting the conditioner soak in. (I really don't make this stuff up.) Here's the passage:

> His divine power has given us everything we need for life
> and godliness through our knowledge of him who called us by

his own glory and goodness. Through these he has given us his very great and precious promises, so that through them you may participate in the divine nature and escape the corruption in the world caused by evil desires.

For this very reason, make every effort to add to your faith goodness; and to goodness, knowledge; and to knowledge, self-control; and to self-control, perseverance; and to perseverance, godliness; and to godliness, brotherly kindness; and to brotherly kindness, love. For if you possess these qualities in increasing measure, they will keep you from being ineffective and unproductive in your knowledge of our Lord Jesus Christ. But if anyone does not have them, he is nearsighted and blind, and has forgotten that he has been cleansed from his past sins.

Well, in the bad old days (back when I thought I was eternally doomed to stay stuck in "the life I didn't sign up for"), I always camped out in verse 3. Here's what I thought it meant: God has given us everything we need, so don't be a brat and ask for more. We've got a free trip to heaven and that's a lot more than a significant percentage of the six billion people currently inhabiting the planet. We have God's Word. We have the freedom to worship God. We have great Bible teaching available through our churches, on radio, TV, audiocassettes, books, etc. Everything we need to grow in godliness is right there for the taking. So go to church, have your quiet time, read through the Bible every year, buy some good Christian books, and quit complaining.

There's a lot of truth in the above paragraph and it's all very fine and good, as far as it goes. It just doesn't go far enough.

Overlooking the Promises

How I managed to overlook verse 4 is a mystery even to me. I guess I had refined the art of editing out those portions of the Bible that didn't fit with my theology or mindset. Here's my big revelation: It is the PROMISES of God that enable us to "participate in the divine nature and escape the corruption in the world." Hello! That's what it says! Duh!

Silly me! I thought it was my good doctrine and my determination to "go and sin no more." Yet there it is: "through them." Through the promises, we find the pathway to pleasing God. How wild is that? Here I thought I was doing God a big favor by not asking him for anything else. You know,

> *Through the promises, we find the pathway to pleasing God.*

God is busy. Besides, I've had my share of blessings—I mean, hey, I don't live in a Third World country, and I eat out once a week— what right do I have to bother him? Yet over and over, God commands us to ask him for what we need—and stuff we just plain old *want*. I'm including a whole series of Scripture passages just in case anyone reading this is as thickheaded as I am. Hard for some of us to believe, but the Bible really does say:

"Ask and it will be given to you; seek and you will find; knock and the door will be opened to you. For everyone who asks receives; he who seeks finds; and to him who knocks, the door will be opened" (Matthew 7:7–8).

"Again, I tell you that if two of you on earth agree about anything you ask for, it will be done for you by my Father in heaven. For where two or three come together in my name, there am I with them" (Matthew 18:19–20).

"Have faith in God," Jesus answered. "I tell you the truth, if anyone says to this mountain, 'Go, throw yourself into the sea,' and does not doubt in his heart but believes that what he says will happen, it will be done for him. Therefore I tell you, whatever you ask for in prayer, believe that you have received it, and it will be yours" (Mark 11:22–24).

"I tell you the truth, my Father will give you whatever you ask in my name. Until now you have not asked for anything in my name. Ask and you will receive, and your joy will be complete" (John 16:23–24).

Dear friends, if our hearts do not condemn us, we have confidence before God and receive from him anything we ask, because we obey his commands and do what pleases him. And this is his command: to believe in the name of his Son, Jesus Christ, and to love one another as he commanded us. Those who obey his commands live in him, and he in them. And this is how we know that he lives in us: We know it by the Spirit he gave us. (1 John 3:21–24)

What Are You Asking For?

I used to look down my spiritual nose at Christians who thought they could go around asking God for whatever they wanted. They just didn't have enough character to be miserable like me! Real Christians aren't into asking for things; we're into suffering, right? Okay, maybe not.

It's taken me twenty-two years to figure out that God really is pleased when we grab hold of his promises. He is pleased when we dare to believe him to do great things. God desires to show himself strong on our behalf. He desires to shower us with good gifts. Let me tell you, folks, this is a whole new approach to the Christian life for me!

Is it possible that the reason you are disappointed with God is because you rarely ask him for anything incredibly wonderful—and as a result, he rarely does anything incredibly wonderful in your life? We are back to the basic spiritual principles that guide the universe. God could just shower you with gifts without your asking. I mean, he's God. Technically speaking, He can do whatever he wants. However, he chooses to act in response to our *faith-filled* prayers. E. M. Bounds, widely recognized as an expert on prayer, has said, "God has chosen to limit his actions on the earth to those things done in direct response to believing prayer."[1] I don't know about you, but that's the most important sentence I've heard in my life. Ponder it. Then put it to the test and see if it isn't so!

> *" God desires to show himself strong on our behalf. He desires to shower us with good gifts. "*

I believe that to a large extent your Christian walk is a reflection

---

[1] As quoted by Dr. Dave Earley, *Basic Training for Spiritual Warfare*, New Life Audios, New Life Community Church. Gahanna, Ohio. For ordering information, call: (614) 475–8500.

of what you are asking God for. All I ever asked God to do was "comfort me in the midst of my suffering." And he did. But until I found within myself the courage to believe God could do more, I was limiting what he could do in my life. If you don't believe God will answer your prayers, you have limited him by your unbelief. Hard to get our brains around that one, but the Bible says it's true. Jesus says to us today the same words he spoke to the two blind men who sought healing two thousand years ago: "According to your faith will it be done to you" (Matthew 9:29). That's not because God loves some Christians more than others; it's not because God is picking on you. It's an inviolable law of the spiritual universe.

For those who have been trapped in a vicious cycle of disappointment and heartache, believing prayer has the power to activate a *positive* cycle of blessing: "Now to him who is able to do immeasurably more than all we ask or imagine, according to his power that is at work within us, to him be glory in the church and in Christ Jesus throughout all generations, for ever and ever! Amen" (Ephesians 3:20–21).

Finding Balance

Now, let's be careful not to turn God into "Our Vending Machine which art in heaven." We cannot get him to do our bidding just by mustering up enough faith. Before you get on your knees and start praying for a new Mercedes, let's come into balance: "You do not have, because you do not ask God. When you ask, you do not receive, because you ask with wrong motives, that you may spend what you get on your pleasures" (James 4:2–3).

Sometimes God loves us so much, he says "no" even if it means risking our disappointment. But that's part of being a good heavenly Father. For example, I love my children with all my heart. When they ask me for things, I try to say "yes" whenever possible. But sometimes I have to love them enough to say "no."

My children don't always understand my reasons, but they are learning to trust me enough to handle the word *no* without falling apart. If they do start falling apart, I'll look them in the eye and say, "Receive the no." That's my way of saying, "It's not what you wanted to hear, but it's what you are hearing anyway, so get over it!"

I have a feeling God routinely says "Receive the no" to his children too. Some of us trust him enough to handle it; others fall apart. Which kind of child are you?

Just this morning God gave me a clear illustration of this principle. You've got to believe me when I tell you I don't make this stuff up! I think God allowed it to hammer home a truth he wants me to share with you. Okay, here goes: *Just this morning,* my twelve-year-old asked if she could drive the car. She wasn't happy when I said she couldn't, but I was extremely happy with how quickly she dropped the subject. That right there is a major triumph, let me tell you!

God isn't interested in raising a bunch of spoiled brats. No, God wants to bless us *so that*—repeat, SO THAT—we can be a blessing to others, which brings us to the second half of the passage. You see, it's all about loving God and loving other people.

Chewing Gum or Bread?

Previously, when I linked together the two paragraphs in this passage (2 Peter 1:3–9), I did it like so: Because "God has given us everything we need" (namely, his Son and his Word) we needed to "make every effort" to develop the character qualities outlined in verses 5 through 9: faith, goodness, knowledge, self-control, perseverance, godliness, brotherly kindness, and love.

Now, this is a little subtle, but it's significant. When I put forth effort toward my spiritual growth, my approach was to study the Scripture, read books, listen to tapes, attend conferences, etc., all with a view toward increasing my knowledge of God, improving my doctrine, and learning how I was supposed to live my life in a way that would please God. And because I was a diligent student, I learned a great deal about the character of God and the history of his dealings with mankind. I learned lots of doctrine and guidelines and rules for Christian living.

Yet despite all my vast storehouse of information, I was *not* becoming more like Jesus. In fact, quite the opposite. I was becoming a rigid, legalistic jerk. (Don't worry about my using the word jerk in a Christian book. It is a biblical term. It comes from the Greek *jerkolopolis*.) It was a long road, but I finally came to the place where I recognized that all my good doctrine had managed to accomplish was to transform me into the kind of person Jesus wouldn't want to spend time with. If our doctrine leads us to reject people Jesus would embrace, then our doctrine is wrong. No matter how many Greek and Hebrew proof-texts you can generate, your doctrine is wrong. Or worse, dangerous to your soul.

Dangerous? How? Because you think you are eating, but you're not! The Word of God wasn't designed to be treated like bubble gum—something you chew on and never digest. Gum is great for blowing bubbles and performing tricks to impress other people. But it doesn't provide any nourishment. It never seeps down into your body to become part of the fabric of your being.

Bread is a whole different food group. The old saying is true: You are what you eat. In this day of rampant bulimia and other eating disorders, it may be necessary for us to rephrase that for greater accuracy: You are what your body digests. I add this clarification because I think there are a great many spiritual bulimics in the church (I was chief among them). A bulimic chews the food, even swallows it, but vomits it back up before it has a chance to digest.

> **"**
>
> *The Word of God wasn't designed to be treated like bubble gum— something you chew on and never digest.*
>
> **"**

Here's how this hazard was described in the outstanding, must-read book *Empowered Evangelicals*:

> One of the occupational hazards of Bible-based churches is bibliolatry [worshiping the Bible rather than God]. The net effect of such bibliolatry is a depersonalization of God. Eventually, we no longer relate to him. God becomes the object of our investigation . . . the vitality of our religion gets sucked out. As God gets dissected, our stance changes from 'I trust in . . .' to 'I believe that. . . ."[2]

---

[2]Rich Nathan and Ken Wilson, *Empowered Evangelicals* (Ann Arbor, Mich.: Vine Books, 1995), 139.

I speak for myself here. I had definitely reduced the Christian life to

- a list of rules I tried to live by, and
- a set of beliefs I gave mental assent to.

Perhaps you've fallen into the same trap. Knowledge about God is not a substitute for a relationship with God. The issue is never "Am I learning more about God?" It is always "Am I becoming more like him?" Unfortunately, I used my list of rules and my set of beliefs as a tool to evaluate *other people*. If they didn't follow the rules or believe the right things, I wrote them off. The more rules I uncovered, the more so-called "truths" I learned, the smaller my list of "approved people" became. The frightening part is there are literally hundreds of thousands of people out there who believe this approach to Christianity is pleasing to God.

> *Knowledge about God is not a substitute for a relationship with God.*

We need balance:

If we emphasize the Word without the Spirit,
    we dry up.
If we emphasize the Spirit without the Word,
    we blow up.
If we hold the Word and the Spirit together,
    we grow up.[3]

---

[3]Nathan and Wilson, *Empowered Evangelicals,* 53.

If you've blown up, you need to get rooted in the Word. If you're drying up, I invite you to consider whether or not you've been guilty of emphasizing the Word without the Spirit—that is, a personal relationship with God is essential, and it is only available through the power of the Holy Spirit living within you.

What's the Bible For?

Last year I attended a four-day Wounded Women conference (a recovery program for women emerging from abusive relationships).[4] At the closing ceremony, each woman was invited forward to receive her graduation certificate and a scroll with a Bible verse. The leader said she had prayed over the scrolls (each of which had a unique message) so that even though we were to reach in and randomly select one, she was confident the Holy Spirit would give us exactly what we needed to hear.

Quite frankly, I was skeptical . . . until I read mine. It was one of those moments when you realize the God of the universe is actually following you around. Slightly unnerving, but glorious at the same time. I tell you, my friends, that little piece of paper hit me like the proverbial two-by-four over the head. It was exactly, word for word, what I needed to hear. Maybe it's what you need to hear, as well:

---

[4] If you are in an abusive relationship or know someone who is, I highly recommend the Wounded Women weekend seminar. Going through their program was a vital part of my healing journey. For more information, contact Wendy Thomas at Word of Grace (480–834–1822).

Ambitious Conqueror:

Jesus said, "You search the Scriptures, for in them you think you have eternal life, but they are that which testify of Me" [John 5:39–40]. So tell Me: Are you searching the Scriptures to learn facts or to learn of Me?

I have called you to friendship, not frenzy. Life, not legalism! Child, seek to know Me, and in knowing Me you will know the truth as well, for truth transcends mere principle in the same way life transcends biological description. The Scriptures will help you to know Me, yes, but only if you meditate upon them with a listening heart.

Love,

Dad

Knowing what the Bible *says* is a great start.

> *The true test of our faith is how we treat other people.*

Knowing what the Bible *means*—that is, having good doctrine—is better.

Knowing how the Bible *applies* to your daily life is better still.

But it's not enough; it must change who we are. I notice a progression in our text for this chapter (2 Peter 1:3–9). We begin to walk by faith and learn to do good things. We increase in knowledge and learn to control our inappropriate behaviors. We learn to persevere in our faith and we become more godly. But ultimately, the true test of our faith is how we treat other people. We must demonstrate brotherly kindness and love, which are the opposite of the selfishness, harshness, and judgmental attitude demonstrated by a depressing number of Christians today. Such people have forgotten that they've been cleansed from past sins. I should know, because I used to be one of them. Not anymore, though, because I'm finding hope and healing.

Without Faith, It Is Impossible to Please God

I think the root of the problem stems from trying to "manufacture" godly character apart from genuine faith. The Scripture says, "Add to your faith." Faith is the cornerstone, the building block upon which all these other character qualities can stand. The Bible plainly says, "Without faith it is impossible to please God" (Hebrews 11:6). Impossible? Wow. Strong words.

So what is faith?

Hebrews 11:1 says, "Now faith is being sure of what we hope for and certain of what we do not see."

And what is faith hoping for?

A reward. In fact, the Bible says anyone who comes to God MUST believe that God is going to reward her! Read it yourself: "Anyone who comes to him must believe that he exists and that he rewards those who earnestly seek him" (Hebrews 11:6).

Let's go back to the beginning of this chapter, when I acknowledged my little insurance policy against disappointment with God. Namely, "Hope for nothing and you'll never be disappointed." That's not faith; it's resignation. That's not hope; it's despair. I was trying to please God by "adding to my resignation and despair." But without faith, it's impossible to please God. I found that out the hard way.

Because try as I might, I could never acquire those other character qualities. In fact, the more I tried and inevitably failed, the more resignation and despair dominated my life.

Like any good writer, God doesn't just *tell* us what faith is; he *shows* us. After defining "faith" in Hebrews 11:1, he devotes the remainder of the chapter to demonstrations of faith in action. "This is what the ancients were commended for" (Hebrews 11:2).

Noah didn't sign up to build an ark. But God asked him to do it, even though there had never been rain on the earth. Noah didn't wait until he saw the floodwaters rising to spring into action. No, "by faith Noah, when warned about things not yet seen, in holy fear built an ark to save his family" (v. 7). Noah spent years building that ark, during which time he was the laughingstock of the neighborhood. And I'm sure there were many days when he was tempted to feel disappointed with God, but he didn't give up. His faith was rewarded when he and his family survived the flood, while the rest of civilization was wiped out.

Abraham didn't sign up to leave his home and virtually all of his relatives to go live in a tent in the middle of nowhere. But God asked him to go. Imagine yourself in the foyer at your church next Sunday: "Yeah, Susan, we're moving."

"Where to?"

"We have no idea. We're just moving."

Faith does that kind of crazy thing—*hoping for the best* and absolutely certain of what it cannot see. "By faith Abraham, when called to go to a place he would later receive as his inheritance, obeyed and went, even though he did not know where he was going" (v. 8).

Abraham never did get a new house, but if he was disappointed with God, he didn't let it show. God gave him the reward he wanted most: a son. My daughter Leah was only seven years old when she turned to me one day and declared, "Mommy, Abraham must have REALLY loved God."

"Why is that, sweetheart?"

"Because he gave him his son *twice*."

Leah doesn't miss much.

Sometimes when I'm speaking at a church I'll stay with a host family rather than in a hotel. It's quite a refreshing change, especially when I know I am truly welcome in the home and I am rewarded with delicious, home-cooked meals. Last February I stayed with a middle-aged couple where the husband absolutely doted upon his wife. You could tell from a mile away how much he adored her. Curious, I asked the wife if it had always been so. "No," she said. "Not until after the cancer." This man's wife nearly died of cancer, but God gave him his wife *twice,* so he was doubly grateful. When I shared with him Leah's insight about Abraham, there were tears in his eyes. This woman didn't sign up for cancer, but she kept the faith and God rewarded her with a second chance at life and a "brand-new" husband.

Sarah didn't sign up to be a barren woman, but God redeemed her tears by giving her a miracle baby in her old age (v. 11). But first he taught her a lesson about laughing when God says he is ready to give us the reward we've wanted for so long.

Moses' parents didn't sign up to surrender their child to the very people who oppressed them as slaves, but their act of faith saved not only the child but an entire nation (v. 23). I can't imagine they are disappointed with God, now that they know how the story ends.

Moses signed up to lead a life of luxury in Pharaoh's palace but wound up spending forty years in the wilderness herding sheep with his father-in-law, and another forty years leading a crowd of complainers through the desert. And after all of that, God forbade him to enter the Promised Land. Moses certainly didn't sign up for any of those disappointments, but he pressed on in faith to the end.

I can't imagine that anyone signed up to be jeered at, tortured, imprisoned, stoned, put to death by sword, or persecuted. But they did not allow the disappointments of life to rob them of their hope and confidence. In the face of all evidence to the contrary, they continued to believe God had something better planned for them (vv. 36–40). And though they didn't get their reward in this lifetime, God is surely lavishing gifts upon them even as we speak. Revelation 2:10 urges us, "Do not be afraid of what you are about to suffer. I tell you, the devil will put some of you in prison to test you, and you will suffer persecution for ten days. Be faithful, even to the point of death, and I will give you the crown of life."

How is it possible that we, who have not faced circumstances nearly so dire, are unwillingly to believe God has something better planned for us? I recently had a friend confront me, very forcefully, with an area of sin in my life. I admitted that I had never taken it very seriously—it went back to my old attitude that God was probably "winking" at my sin. My unspoken goal, in so many areas of my life, had always been to see "how much I could get away with and still sneak into heaven." Now, at last, someone had the guts to call me on it. She said, "Don't you realize that you're cheating your-self? Don't you realize that someday we will be rewarded for our faithfulness? Isn't it real to you that we will reign with God through-out all eternity and that our place in that kingdom will be deter-mined by how faithful we are in this life?"

Actually, no. It had never been real to me before. But as she looked intently at me with tears in her eyes, a giant light bulb went on over my head. There really IS a coming kingdom. I really WILL be rewarded if I continue to walk by faith and live a life that is honoring to God. Every time I "do the bare minimum" or "try to get away with something," I am robbing myself. If we really have faith in God, no matter how disappointing our life has been thus far, we *must* remain "sure of what we hope for and certain of what we do not see." We must believe that God has a reward for us, both in this life and in the coming kingdom.

> *"*
>
> *Every time I "do the bare minimum" or "try to get away with something," I am robbing myself.*
>
> *"*

A Word About Tragedy

I want to say a word about tragedy, but I don't want to say too much because I feel unqualified to speak. True, I've had my share of heartache—but all of my pain can be traced back to human choices. Either mine or someone else's. Yet I know there are times in this life when no human explanation can be found.

Margie Erbe knows about tragedy. Margie was miraculously healed of a brain tumor, then lived through hell on earth learning to function again as an adult human being. But God saw her through the experience, then led her into a speaking and writing ministry. She was invited to speak at Arrowhead Ranch, the international headquarters of Campus Crusade for Christ—which is a great honor for a speaker. God told her, very clearly, that this event would be a turning point in her life.

Turning point? she thought. *How exciting. I'm going to bring the whole family.* Shortly after she gave her testimony concerning how God had allowed her to triumph over tragedy, her thirteen-year-old son, Danny, went inline-skating around the campus.

He fell, right there on the holy ground of Arrowhead Ranch.

He fell, hit his head . . . and he died.

I remember Margie calling me early one morning. She didn't say hello. She said, "Danny's dead."

I remember attending the funeral. I remember Margie looking me straight in the eyes—looking straight through me—on her way out of the church. I remember it like it happened two seconds ago.

I had nothing to say then. Nothing to say now.

Instead, let me introduce someone who *does* have something profound to say. Philip Yancey, in his amazing book *Disappointment With God*, quotes his friend Douglas, who has severe debilitating headaches from a car accident:

I have learned to see beyond the physical reality in this world to the spiritual reality. We tend to think, "Life should be fair because God is fair." But God is not life. And if I confuse God with the physical reality of life—by expecting constant good health, for example—then I set myself up for a crashing disappointment. God's existence, even his love for me, does not depend on my good health. Frankly, I've had more time and opportunity to work on my relationship with God during my impairment than before.[5]

I once worked with a woman who was pregnant with twins. It had been a few years since I'd last seen her, when I bumped into her on the street and enthusiastically inquired about the children. "They both died," she said quietly. "One of the babies lived for eight hours. I treasure the memory of holding her. It was the most precious experience of my life." Thankfully, I was rendered speechless.

My sister works at St. Christopher's Hospital for Children in Philadelphia. The mere thought that there are entire buildings dedicated to sick and dying children is almost more than I can bear. Her area of expertise is hematology-oncology. That is, she works with children with cancer and blood disorders like leukemia and AIDS. Now, with AIDS, we might occasionally be able to point the finger at a drug-addicted parent and "comfort" ourselves that the universe still makes sense. However, most of the suffering she witnesses on a daily basis is inexplicable.

I never have theological discussions with my sister. She says the parents clutching Bibles don't survive any better than the parents

---

[5]Philip Yancey, *Disappointment With God* (Grand Rapids, Mich.: Zondervan Publishing House, 1988), 183.

who are merely clutching each other. I guess clutching a Bible and being in its clutches are two different things.

> Saints become saints by somehow hanging on to the stubborn conviction that things are not as they appear, and that the unseen world is as solid and trustworthy as the visible world around them. God deserves trust, even when it looks like the world is caving in. "The world was not worthy of them," Hebrews 11 concludes about its amazing assemblage, adding this intriguing comment: "Therefore God is not ashamed to be called their God."[6]

But here's the main point I want to make. My sister says—and she of all people should know—tragedy merely "brings out what's already there." It doesn't make the parents stronger. If they are strong, they survive. If they aren't strong, they fall apart. "Some people blame God," she says. "Some people doubt God. The smart ones *thank* God for allowing them to experience whatever time they DID have with their child."

How Character Is Transformed

I used to think hardship was the best way to build character. I was wrong. It's certainly one way, but it's not the most effective way. (Yet another brain torque for those of us who specialize in learning everything through painful experience.) The best way to build our

---

[6]Ibid., 205.

character is in meditation upon the promises of God, convincing our hearts of his goodness. That way, if and when tragedy does strike, we will endure. And this much I know for sure: two months of such meditation has done more to transform my personality than twenty years of look-it-up-and-find-the-right-answer Bible study.

Yancey concludes, "If we insist on visible proofs from God, we may well prepare the way for a permanent state of disappointment. True faith does not so much attempt to manipulate God to do our will as it does to position us to do his will."[7] We are not transformed by rising to the occasion. We rise to the occasion because we have been transformed. How are we transformed? By the renewing of our mind. By convincing our heart that God is good, even when our circumstances are not.

> **"** *We are not transformed by rising to the occasion. We rise to the occasion because we have been transformed.* **"**

---

[7]Ibid., 241.

I ~~Signed~~ UP FOR HAPPINESS

CHAPTER SIX

I Signed Up for Happiness

My daughter Leah disappeared for several hours one day last summer. Since she's a homeschooled nature lover, I wasn't completely surprised that she had ventured off outdoors. When she finally came back into the house, I could tell she was excited about some new discovery. "Where've you been?" I asked.

"Watching an anthill," she declared. "Ants are so amazing, Mom! They never stop. You should have seen one of them carrying a great big sunflower seed. *The queen's own children work themselves to death for her!*"

This child's insight never ceases to amaze me. As she stood there breathless in the kitchen, it occurred to me that a lot of *the King's own children* are working themselves to death for him. And when we stop, we feel guilty. Funny thing, though, unlike the queen ant, God doesn't want his children on the run.

If you're anything like me, my guess is you're on the run more often than not. Lots of people, especially good, upstanding Christian people, feel compelled to run around like busy little creatures. It makes us feel important. But it doesn't make us very happy, does it?

I'm quite certain that God would much rather have us sitting at his feet than running self-assigned errands for him. I've made it my goal never to mention Martha or Mary (Luke 10:38–42) in my books, but if I were to mention them, it would be right here. And I think you can pretty much guess what I would say.

Again, in contrast to the queen ant, God doesn't want us carrying giant loads. Instead, he says:

> "Come to me, all you who are weary and burdened, and I will give you rest. Take my yoke upon you and learn from me, for I am gentle and humble in heart, and you will find rest for your souls. For my yoke is easy and my burden is light" (Matthew 11:28–30).

His Feet or Someone Else's Door

The problem with carrying around heavy loads is that eventually you've got to set them down somewhere. Or in my case, I used to set them down everywhere. No one could get within a mile of me without hearing a litany of my complaints. The kids weren't listening. I couldn't keep up with my credit card bills. Life on the road was exhausting me; or alternatively, my ministry was in the tank and I wasn't spending enough time on the road. No one loved me anymore. I hated my house. (You know, the one I begged God to give me.) I couldn't keep it and I couldn't sell it. My dog ran away. My car broke down. On and on it went. Negative. Negative. Negative.

Yet I couldn't figure out why my phone never rang. All I wanted to do was spread the misery around. I was doing people a favor, helping them stay in touch with "the real world."

I had one person in particular I liked to complain to because she not only listened sympathetically, she would add little commentary that confirmed she knew the magnitude of my suffering. I'll call her Cindy. I figured it was good for Cindy to listen to my woes since she always had a great big smile on her face and obviously had life "made in the shade." I mean, she never indicated having any problems of her own.

Then one day a mutual friend mentioned in passing that Cindy was dying. "Dying?" I looked at her in astonishment. "As in *dying* dying? But she's only in her forties. How is that possible?" It turns out that Cindy had contracted an incurable disease some five years ago and has been battling it ever since. Cindy is dying. But Cindy is remarkably happy. Unlike me, even though I am not dying and have nothing like her excuse to be unhappy.

Cindy never once mentioned her terminal illness to me in between my sorrowful tales of burnt toast and credit card bills. Although she did share this sage advice with me one day: "You know, Donna, everybody has their own bag of rocks to carry."

And I started to think about that. Everyone has their own bag of rocks. Everyone has their own war stories. Their own heartaches. What right do I have to ask other people to carry *my* bag in addition to their own? What right did I have to burden down this dying woman with my never-ending negativity?

No right at all. That's why Jesus told us to lay our burdens down at his feet, to make it easier for us to resist the temptation to lay them down at everyone else's door.

How Happy Do You Want to Be?

You know how sometimes you hear a pithy little expression and you wish you hadn't? I once heard it said, "Most people are pretty much as happy as they've made up their minds to be." Ouch. I didn't like that at all. 'Cause, frankly, I was miserable. And it's bad enough to be miserable without being blamed for your own misery.

Wouldn't you know, it turns out to be true? The world is a great big place, and our experience of the world hinges on one very simple decision we make every day: what will we focus on? We can choose to focus on what's wrong with the world and be miserable. Or we can choose to focus on what's right with the world and be happy.

> "
> *We can choose to focus on what's right with the world and be happy.*
> "

Cindy hops out of bed in the morning and says, "I'm alive today. That's a good thing. I'm happy about that." I drag myself out of bed and say, "I have fat thighs. That's a bad thing. I'm unhappy about that."

Two women. Two choices. One happy. The other unhappy.

Life is a funny thing.

Magnifying Glass

Imagine that you are standing next to a gigantic poster filled with a wide variety of tiny little images—some beautiful, some frightening; some bright, some dark. Now imagine that you have a magnifying glass in your hand. What will determine the type of images you see? Where you point your magnifying glass.

Every moment of every day has good and bad in it. Every person you meet has strengths and weaknesses. Every situation has pros and cons. Every event contains both the handiwork of God and the counterattack of the enemy. Even "the life you didn't sign up for" is filled with things you *did* sign up for, when you stop and think about it.

The question is: What will you choose to magnify? It's entirely up to you. Keep in mind: Whatever you focus your magnifying glass on will appear larger than everything else. When you choose to magnify the bad, it appears larger than it really is. But when you choose to magnify God, you get a clearer picture of reality. You realize that God is larger than your problems. Here's how the psalmist put it:

> I will bless the Lord at all times;
> His praise shall continually be in my mouth.
> My soul shall make its boast in the Lord;
> The humble shall hear of it and be glad.
> Oh, *magnify* the Lord with me,
> And let us exalt His name together.
>
> I sought the Lord, and He heard me,
> And delivered me from all my fears.

They looked to Him and were radiant,
And their faces were not ashamed.
This poor man cried out, and the Lord heard him,
And saved him out of all his troubles.
The angel of the Lord encamps all around those who fear Him,
And delivers them.

Oh, taste and see that the Lord is good;
Blessed is the man who trusts in Him!
Oh, fear the Lord, you His saints!
There is no want to those who fear Him.
The young lions lack and suffer hunger;
But those who seek the Lord shall not lack any good thing.

Come, you children, listen to me;
I will teach you the fear of the Lord.
Who is the man who desires life,
And loves many days, that he may see good?
Keep your tongue from evil,
And your lips from speaking deceit.
Depart from evil and do good;
Seek peace and pursue it.

The eyes of the Lord are on the righteous,
And His ears are open to their cry.
The face of the Lord is against those who do evil,
To cut off the remembrance of them from the earth.

The righteous cry out, and the Lord hears,
And delivers them out of all their troubles.
The Lord is near to those who have a broken heart,
And saves such as have a contrite spirit.

Many are the afflictions of the righteous,
But the Lord delivers him out of them all.
He guards all his bones;
Not one of them is broken.
Evil shall slay the wicked,
And those who hate the righteous shall be condemned.
The Lord redeems the soul of His servants,
And none of those who trust in Him shall be condemned.

    (Psalm 34 NKJV)

Webster's Dictionary defines *magnify*: "to make great in representation; to extol; to exalt in description or praise. To elevate; to raise in estimation; to increase the apparent dimensions." *The New International Version* of the Bible renders the word *magnify* as "exalt," which *Webster's* defines: "to elevate with joy or confidence."

When you choose to magnify God rather than your problems, you elevate God with joy and confidence. Isn't that perfect? Not in resignation. Not as a Pollyanna, who denies the reality of the situation. Instead, with confidence in God's goodness, you can approach life in a healthy, balanced way that acknowledges the heartaches and disappointments of life but still chooses to see God's redemptive power at work.

Complaining

The opposite of magnifying God is complaining. It has been observed that "complaining is like whistling for the devil." So unless you want the enemy to show up on your doorstep, you'd better stop complaining. The first time I took the sin of complaining seriously was when I read the following passage and realized how seriously God takes it:

> Now the people complained about their hardships in the hearing of the Lord, and when he heard them his anger was aroused. Then fire from the Lord burned among them and consumed some of the outskirts of the camp. When the people cried out to Moses, he prayed to the Lord and the fire died down. So that place was called Taberah, because fire from the Lord had burned among them.
>
> The rabble with them began to crave other food, and again the Israelites started wailing and said, "If only we had meat to eat! We remember the fish we ate in Egypt at no cost—also the cucumbers, melons, leeks, onions and garlic. But now we have lost our appetite; we never see anything but this manna!"
>
> The manna was like coriander seed and looked like resin. The people went around gathering it, and then ground it in a handmill or crushed it in a mortar. They cooked it in a pot or made it into cakes. And it tasted like something made with olive oil. When the dew settled on the camp at night, the manna also came down.
>
> Moses heard the people of every family wailing, each at the entrance to his tent. The Lord became exceedingly angry, and Moses was troubled. He asked the Lord, "Why have you brought this trouble on your servant? What have I done to displease you that you put the burden of all these people on me? Did I conceive all these people? Did I give them birth? Why do you tell me to carry them in my arms, as a nurse carries an

infant, to the land you promised on oath to their forefathers? Where can I get meat for all these people? They keep wailing to me, 'Give us meat to eat!' I cannot carry all these people by myself; the burden is too heavy for me. If this is how you are going to treat me, put me to death right now—if I have found favor in your eyes—and do not let me face my own ruin" (Numbers 11:1–15).

Notice how complaining affects the people around us who are trying to keep a positive attitude. Other people's complaining made Moses so miserable he wanted to die. He had too many people asking him to carry their "bag of rocks."

God takes our complaints seriously, and he takes them personally. In Philippians 2:14–16, he commands us:

Do everything without complaining or arguing, so that you may become blameless and pure, children of God without fault in a crooked and depraved generation, in which you shine like stars in the universe as you hold out the word of life—in order that I may boast on the day of Christ that I did not run or labor for nothing.

The Power of Affirmations

Recently a friend encouraged me to compile a list of daily affirmations—positive words I speak aloud that reflect not where I am right now but where I want to go and who I want to be. It's been a wonderful addition to my prayer time each day. I feel confident that

I am becoming a happier person as a result of this simple exercise. Let me share some of my affirmations with you. They are very personal—I'm really giving you a glimpse into the deepest desires of my heart here. If you are ever wondering how you might pray effectively for me, you can pray that I would truly become the woman described below, even as you pray that these things would be true in your own life:

- I know today will be a great day, because God's mercies are new every morning. (Lamentations 3:23)
- No weapon that's formed against me today will prosper. All those who rise up against me will fall. Every accusation made against me will be refuted. (Isaiah 54:17)
- The enemy may come against me one way, but he'll be forced to flee from me seven ways! (Deuteronomy 28:7)
- Today I will know firsthand the love of Christ, which passes knowledge, and I will be filled with the fullness of God. (Ephesians 3:19)
- I'm not going to be afraid of anything today. Because God has not given me a spirit of fear but of love, power, and a sound mind. (2 Timothy 1:7)
- I can either magnify God or magnify my problems. I choose to magnify God. (Psalm 69:30–31)
- This family is blessed when we come in and blessed when we go out. (Deuteronomy 28:6)
- I have absolutely no regrets about my life. Everything that's happened to me, even the pain, will be redeemed and turned into

something good. (Romans 8:28)

- I never complain, because I refuse to whistle for the devil. (Philippians 2:14)

- I never complain, because it robs me—and everyone around me—of joy. Besides, the world doesn't need any more verbal pollution. (Philippians 2:14)

- I always remember: She who guards her mouth and her tongue keeps herself from trouble. (Proverbs 21:23)

- I always choose to offer the sacrifice of praise and thanksgiving (Hebrews 13:15). God inhabits praise. The enemy inhabits negativity. I can choose who I cohabit with. I choose God.

- I never make excuses for my behavior. All that does is keep me stuck. (1 John 1:8–9)

- I know that life and death are in the power of the tongue. So I let the words of my mouth and the meditation of my heart be acceptable before God. (Psalm 19:14)

- I never judge anyone, because I know everyone is doing the very best they can. (Matthew 7:1)

- I never curse or condemn anyone, because I want to keep God's blessings flowing into my life. (Luke 6:37)

- If people could sum me up in one word, they would say: gracious. I always extend to others the same grace God has extended to me. (Ephesians 4:29–32)

- I am becoming more and more like Jesus all the time: gracious, generous, anointed, and compassionate. I walk moment by moment in the power of the Holy Spirit. (2 Corinthians 3:17–18)

Re-creating Atmosphere

I believe the reason my daily recitation of affirmations is having such a powerful impact on my life is because it is resetting my emotional thermostat. Let me explain. You know how a thermostat works, right? You set it to 70 degrees or whatever temperature feels most comfortable for you. Then when the temperature in the room reaches above or drops below that point, the air-conditioning/heating unit automatically kicks in to bring the room back to the selected temperature.

Our emotional thermostats are set at a very young age. If you grew up in a quiet, peaceful, loving home, your temperature is probably set around 68 degrees. Not too hot. Not too cold. That's one of the reasons why people raised in Christian homes—and especially those whose families have been believers for generations—have very peaceful lives. (There are other reasons, which I discussed at length in my book *Standing Firm* [Bethany House, 2001], but the emotional thermostat is certainly significant.)

However, if you were raised in a non-believing home, especially if it was a home filled with chaos and conflict, your emotional thermostat is set around 85 degrees. Maybe even higher. And this is the key: When life cools down a bit, something inside of you will *automatically* kick in to raise the temperature. You will unconsciously look for ways to heat things up! To stir up trouble. To get that adrenaline rushing. You re-create the atmosphere that feels most familiar.

I did this constantly. If I didn't have a crisis, I'd invent one. If I wasn't embroiled in conflict with someone, I'd pick a fight. I was always poised for battle. As a result, I invariably managed to find a worthy opponent. If I didn't have something at the moment to make me unhappy, I would look for something to be unhappy about.

I was continually in a state of turmoil, continually working myself into a frenzy, but God has clearly called me—just as he has called you—to reset the thermostat to a peaceful temperature. He has called us to quietness and rest. He has called us to happiness.

> I don't want you to work for Me under pressure and tension like a machine—striving to produce, produce. I want you to just LIVE with ME as a PERSON. I have waited for you to wear yourself out. I knew you would find it eventually—the secret of silence and rest, of solitude and of song. I will rebuild your strength—not to work again in foolish frenzy, but just for the sake of making you strong and well. To Me this is an end in itself. Make it your aim and join with Me wholeheartedly in this project. Many joys are waiting yet.[1]

Do you believe many joys are waiting for you? Indeed, you are surrounded by a multitude of people and places that could fill your heart with happiness every day. All you have to do is open your eyes and see the good. Right now, you can choose to enjoy the happiness you signed up for. What are you waiting for?

---

[1]Roberts, *Come Away, My Beloved,* 152.

I

Signed

UP FOR

GREAT

HEALTH

I Signed Up for Great Health

In one sense, I am completely unqualified to write this chapter, because I have been chronically sick for twenty years. Even though I don't have a life-threatening illness, I am frequently "under the weather," and often I'm flat-out "down for the count." In recent years I have had two different occasions where friends showed up at my house and found me delirious with fevers hovering around 104 degrees. One of these women told a mutual friend she'd never seen anyone look so near death in her life.

In another sense, I am eminently qualified to write about it because I know what it feels like to be sick all the time. If you're anything like me, you are sick and tired of feeling sick and tired. Or maybe someone in your life is chronically ill and your life has been profoundly affected by their suffering.

I wanted you to know up front that I have not yet discovered the great health I signed up for. But I'm a whole lot healthier than I used to be, and that right there is something to celebrate. Although this chapter will not be definitive by any stretch of the imagination, I'd like to share with you what God has shown me about the various causes of sickness, along with the prescription I am pursuing in my own life. Maybe together we can discover the path to the great health we signed up for.

The Suffering of Job

Quoting from the book of Job is always a tricky business because more than half of the dialogue is included for the express purpose of exposing wrong-headed thinking. I don't know about you, but that makes me fear quoting it in some wrong-headed fashion. But how cowardly can I be? To write an entire book entitled *This Isn't the Life I Signed Up For* and not tackle Job? Tsk. Tsk. So while I am quaking in my boots, we shall read a selection together:

> On another day the angels came to present themselves before the Lord, and Satan also came with them to present himself before him. And the Lord said to Satan, "Where have you come from?"
>
> Satan answered the Lord, "From roaming through the earth and going back and forth in it."
>
> Then the Lord said to Satan, "Have you considered my servant Job? There is no one on earth like him; he is blameless and upright, a man who fears God and shuns evil. And he still maintains his integrity, though you incited me against him to ruin him without any reason."
>
> "Skin for skin!" Satan replied. "A man will give all he has for

his own life. But stretch out your hand and strike his flesh and bones, and he will surely curse you to your face."

The Lord said to Satan, "Very well, then, he is in your hands; but you must spare his life."

So Satan went out from the presence of the Lord and afflicted Job with painful sores from the soles of his feet to the top of his head. Then Job took a piece of broken pottery and scraped himself with it as he sat among the ashes.

His wife said to him, "Are you still holding on to your integrity? Curse God and die!"

He replied, "You are talking like a foolish woman. Shall we accept good from God, and not trouble?" (Job 2:1–10).

Sickness Can Be Due to Satanic Affliction

Before launching into this, let me say that I'm in the enviable position of not having a theological ax to grind. There will be something in the following paragraphs for everyone to dispute. It's not important for you to agree with me; what matters is that you begin to get God's perspective and move a step closer to experiencing "the life you signed up for." All I'm asking is that you prayerfully consider what I'm about to say.

When the Bible tells us something clearly, we don't need to start reading between the lines or trying to explain things away because they make us uncomfortable. In this case, the Bible tells us *exactly* what happened. Job was the most righteous man living on the earth at the time. Satan asked for permission to afflict him and God granted him that permission, even though God himself says Job had done nothing wrong to provoke it. "Satan went out from the presence of the Lord and AFFLICTED Job with painful sores from the soles of his feet to the top of his head" (Job 2:7, emphasis added). Obviously Satan has the power to afflict people with sickness. He can even afflict nice, upstanding Christians. And God lets him do it. I don't understand it. I don't particularly like it. But that's what it says.

Jesus himself addressed the difficult and perplexing issue of human suffering:

> As He went along, He saw a man blind from birth. His disciples asked Him, "Rabbi, who sinned, this man or his parents, that he was born blind?"
>
> "Neither this man nor his parents sinned," said Jesus, "but this happened so that the work of God might be displayed in his life" (John 9:1–3).

Jesus clearly states that sickness is NOT always the result of sin, as some teachers today claim. Sometimes God allows physical disability for a specific purpose. In this instance, this man's life demonstrated to the Pharisees (and whoever else would listen) that spiritual blindness is worse than physical blindness. Physical blindness is temporary, but spiritual blindness is eternal hell.

The following example of a physical handicap for God's glory is written by Arthur Christopher Bacon and quoted by L. B. Cowman in her devotional book *Streams in the Desert* (February 12):[1]

---

[1]L. B. Cowman, *Streams in the Desert* (Grand Rapids, Mich.: Zondervan Publishing House, 1999—updated).

A visitor at a school for the deaf was writing questions on the board for the children. Soon he wrote this sentence: "Why has God made me able to hear and speak, and made you deaf?"

The shocking sentence hit the children like a cruel slap on the face. They sat paralyzed, pondering the dreadful word "Why?" And a little girl arose. With her eyes swimming with tears, she walked straight to the board. Picking up the chalk, she wrote with a steady hand these precious words: "Yes, Father, for this was your good pleasure" (Matthew 11:26). What a reply! It reaches up and claims an eternal truth upon which the most mature believer, and even the youngest child of God, may securely rest—the truth that God is your Father.

Is All Suffering Noble?

I grew up believing that suffering of any kind—including sickness—was inherently noble. It was a badge of honor, a form of martyrdom. It was a sign that you were a giant of the faith, like Job, because God knew he could entrust you with suffering and you wouldn't "curse God and die." I once heard a message entitled "Can God Trust You?" and it really had an impact on me. *Yes,* I thought. *I want to be someone God can trust. I don't want to be a fair-weather friend of God, who only accepts good from his hand and not trouble.* I'm glad I heard that message and took it to heart. I think it's made me a better person, less of a spiritual wimp than I otherwise would have been. But I think I took it to the extreme and passively accepted suffering that God never intended me to endure. I tended to lie down and die, when God wanted me to stand and fight.

Although no one came out and said so, of course, I've attended churches where the most admired people were those who suffered the most. This theological line of thought is rooted in the book of Job. God deliberately brings Job to Satan's attention as a stellar example of faithfulness. God says, in essence, "Of all my servants, this is one you can put to the test, because I know he will do me proud." So whenever we saw Christians who were sick or suffering, we assumed that a similar conversation had taken place in heaven, with God saying to Satan, "There's another of my best and brightest. Go put her to the test."

The New Testament also lends support to this perspective:

> Consider it pure joy, my brothers, whenever you face trials of many kinds, because you know that the testing of your faith develops perseverance. Perseverance must finish its work so that you may be mature and complete, not lacking anything. (James 1:2–4)

Even Jesus was not exempt from suffering (although it's interesting to note there is no mention in Scripture of Jesus experiencing sickness):

> During the days of Jesus' life on earth, he offered up prayers and petitions with loud cries and tears to the one who could save him from death, and he was heard because of his reverent submission. Although he was a son, he learned obedience from what he suffered and, once made perfect, he became the source of eternal salvation for all who obey him. (Hebrews 5:7–9)

The Exception or the Rule?

Clearly God sometimes allows sickness and physical disability. And it's equally clear that such suffering brings out the best in some people. They seize the opportunity to find God in the midst of their pain. But let's be honest and come into balance here: Chronic illness can also warp our character rather than build it. For every Joni Eareckson Tada, there are hundreds of self-consumed sick people whose only topic of conversation is their current symptoms. I should know, because that's exactly what happened to me. My chronic illness did not turn my eyes toward God; it turned my gaze inward. Proverbs 18:14 points out, "A man's spirit sustains him in sickness, but a crushed spirit who can bear?" In other words, it can really wear you down after a while. Or, as mentioned previously, suffering of any variety often brings to the surface what is already inside of us. That's why the Scripture says, "Above all else, guard your heart, for it is the wellspring of life" (Proverbs 4:23).

Although there are obvious exceptions (as noted above), the lives of God's favored children throughout the Old Testament were typically characterized by health and long life. Throughout Scripture, sickness is frequently portrayed not as a test of faithfulness but as a curse or the consequence of disobedience. When the Israelites entered the Promised Land, God warned them about this very thing:

> If you do not carefully follow all the words of this law, which are written in this book, and do not revere this glorious and awesome name—the Lord your God—the Lord will send fearful plagues on you and your descendants, harsh and

prolonged disasters, and severe and lingering illnesses. He will bring upon you all the diseases of Egypt that you dreaded, and they will cling to you. The Lord will also bring on you every kind of sickness and disaster not recorded in this Book of the Law, until you are destroyed. You who were as numerous as the stars in the sky will be left but few in number, because you did not obey the Lord your God. Just as it pleased the Lord to make you prosper and increase in number, so it will please him to ruin and destroy you. (Deuteronomy 28:58–63)

> "
>
> *"Far better to be made holy through prayer and Bible reading, fellowship, worship and obedience to the commandments of God."*
>
> "

The above passage clearly says sickness is sometimes sent as a punishment for disobedience. Now don't panic. I didn't say always. I said sometimes.

I've heard people say that God allowed an illness—or even that he sent an illness—in order to get their attention so that they would make changes in their lives. Although it is certainly true that sickness often forces us to stop and take a hard look at our lives, wouldn't it be better to look before we wound up in a hospital bed? As the authors of *Empowered Evangelicals* put it, "Far better to be made holy through prayer and Bible reading, fellowship, worship and obedience to the commandments of God than through the brokenness caused by the fall."[2]

---

[2]Nathan and Wilson, *Empowered Evangelicals*, 80.

The following passages are typical of the lifestyle of Jesus:

> Jesus went throughout Galilee, teaching in their synagogues, preaching the good news of the kingdom, and healing every disease and sickness among the people. (Matthew 4:23)
>
> Jesus went through all the towns and villages, teaching in their synagogues, preaching the good news of the kingdom and healing every disease and sickness. (Matthew 9:35)
>
> When the sun was setting, the people brought to Jesus all who had various kinds of sickness, and laying his hands on each one, he healed them. (Luke 4:40)

I can't help but notice what these verses *don't* say. They don't say Jesus went around making people sick so they could prove how much faith they had or to get their attention. Quite the opposite. He made it one of his primary missions to heal people and repeatedly said, "Your faith has made you well" (Luke 17:19). He never once said, "Your faith has allowed you to get sick."

There is a single instance where Jesus apparently allowed someone to get sick and die and it was done for the express purpose of glorifying God. But notice, it was not the sickness (and ultimate death) that glorified God; it was the healing and resurrection that glorified God:

> Now a man named Lazarus was sick. He was from Bethany, the village of Mary and her sister Martha. This Mary, whose brother Lazarus now lay sick, was the same one who poured perfume on the Lord and wiped his feet with her hair. So the sisters sent word to Jesus, "Lord, the one you love is sick."

When he heard this, Jesus said, "This sickness will not end in death. No, it is for God's glory so that God's Son may be glorified through it" (John 11:1–4). [As I'm sure you know, Lazarus died and Jesus raised him from the dead.]

Is Sickness the Result of a Lack of Faith?

So what shall we conclude? Clearly Jesus had a passion for healing the sick. And since he is the same yesterday, today, and forever, we can be certain he still desires to heal the sick among us. I think it's obvious that a loving heavenly Father would generally want his children to be healthy, just as a loving earthly father would. Can you imagine a parent injecting her child with the flu to "teach him a lesson" or to "get his attention"? Certainly not! What do we think of parents who deliberately inflict pain on their children? We lock them up as child abusers.

Here again, Christians go to extremes. Some teach that if we have enough faith, we will never be sick throughout our entire lifetime. If we are sick, there is invariably a lack of faith involved. But what can we say about a three-year-old girl dying of leukemia? That she has somehow committed some wicked deed? Impossible! Or that she's being punished for the sins of her parents? Well then, why are the babies found in trash cans invariably healthy? If God were going to punish wickedness with birth defects, these people would be giving birth to seriously deformed kids. Can we say that she or her parents lack faith? Plenty of atheists and agnostics give birth to healthy children, so it's hardly a cause-effect relationship.

I once attended a Bible study with a young woman who'd been left devastated after her baby was born ancephalic, that is, without a brain. But her church said if she had enough faith, her baby would live. She believed with all her heart that God was going to perform a mighty miracle, but her baby died. Sadly, she lost not only her baby but also her "standing" in the church. She almost lost her grip on sanity, not to mention her faith.

Lack of faith is not the only explanation for the heartaches of life. It definitely explains some things . . . but not all. Repeat: Lack of faith is not the only explanation for the heartaches of life. It definitely explains some things . . . but not all.

> *80 percent of all church prayer requests are related to sickness.*

What I'm trying to advocate here is some kind of balance . . . and may God help me! I know I'm walking into the middle of the fray. I was tempted to delete this entire chapter, because I know I'm stepping all over people's toes. But how could I possibly discuss "the life I didn't sign up for" without addressing sickness? A national Christian magazine surveyed pastors and discovered that 80 percent of all church prayer requests are related to sickness. My own sense, just from twenty-two years hanging around church, is that this estimate is accurate. So we need to get a grip on this issue.

It would seem to me that the healthiest view of sickness (if you'll pardon the pun) is to view it "chiefly as a consequence of the . . . universal human experience of fallenness and not primarily as being sent to us by God to make us holy"[3] Nor as a result of a lack of faith on our part.

We live in a fallen world, not the best of all possible worlds. The Garden of Eden is a distant memory. Today the garden is filled with pesticides, not to mention the fallout of nuclear bombs and other toxic waste. In my own case, I grew up playing in a wooded lot near my home that was later declared a "Super-Fund Site" by the Environmental Protection Agency (meaning it was so toxic, it was a top priority for cleanup). My extended family is riddled with cancer, but I sincerely doubt the cause is a family curse or lack of faith. A more likely explanation is that we lived in a highly industrial area of the Northeast.

Shortly after writing the above paragraph, I stumbled upon the following article on the Internet:

> Long-term exposure to the air pollution in some of America's biggest metropolitan areas significantly raises the risk of dying from lung cancer and is about as dangerous as living with a smoker, a study of a half-million people found. The study echoes previous research and provides the strongest evidence yet of the health dangers of the pollution levels found in many big cities and even some smaller ones, according to the researchers from Brigham Young University and New York University.[4]

---

[3]Ibid., 80.
[4]Associated Press report on the Internet, March 5, 2002.

No doubt about it, folks. We live in a fallen world, and that has major ramifications for our health.

Sickness Can Be a Logical Consequence of Our Lifestyle

In many instances, sickness is nothing more than the logical consequence of our lifestyle. We don't need to look for profound supernatural explanations when plain old common sense will do. I'm not going to devote too much time to this point, because I think it is self-explanatory. Nevertheless, it is extremely significant. Don't let the length of the paragraph fool you into underestimating its importance. Poor diet and lack of exercise account for a wide range of common ailments. Many people neglect their physical body, then blame God or the devil when they become ill. If you are fifty pounds overweight and think lifting the potato chip from the bag to your mouth is a workout, you don't need to ponder whether or not Satan is afflicting you. You are afflicting yourself. And there is nothing noble about that kind of suffering.

I recently received an e-mail from a woman who has totally turned her life around by changing her lifestyle. In January 2001, she attended one of my conferences and e-mailed me afterward, telling me her marriage was in trouble. I felt led to ask her how she felt about herself. "Terrible," was the response. She was overweight and chronically sick. Apparently I inspired her to undertake the Body for Life program, which I mentioned in my previous book *Standing Firm*. She lost fifty-five pounds, saved her marriage, and says she has never felt better in her life. I am quite certain one of the factors in my chronic sickness is my addiction to carbohydrates, coupled with my aversion to vegetables. God has convicted me that it's not enough to pray for healing; I have to modify my eating habits. My guess is that nine out of ten women reading this could benefit by a change in their diet and exercise habits.

Sickness Can Be Rooted in Emotional Pain

There are other ways to abuse our physical bodies besides neglecting exercise. Medical science continues to confirm that many illnesses are rooted in emotional pain, which manifests itself in physical pain. There are exceptions, of course, but many diseases can be traced back to anxiety and stress. Long-term, low-level anxiety has been directly linked to cancer. High levels of stress are clearly the primary cause of heart attacks. I recently read an alarming statistic about the number of women in abusive relationships who contract breast cancer. Other studies have linked breast cancer to post-abortion syndrome. That's not to say that all breast cancer victims are in abusive relationships or have endured the heartbreak of abortion, but who can deny that emotional pain eventually takes a toll on the body?

God has created us as triune creatures: spirit, soul, and body. First Thessalonians 5:23 says, "May your whole spirit, soul and body be kept blameless at the coming of our Lord Jesus Christ." And 2 Corinthians 7:1 reminds us, "Since we have these promises, dear friends, let us purify ourselves from everything that contaminates body and spirit, perfecting holiness out of reverence for God."

Whatever impacts one part of our being impacts the other two parts as well. If we neglect our spirit, our soul and body suffer. If we neglect our soul (that is, our mind, will, and emotions), our spirit and body suffer. And if we neglect our body, it typically has a *negative—not positive*—effect on our spirit and soul. Isn't that just common sense?

> **"**
>
> *Many diseases can be traced back to anxiety and stress.*
>
> **"**

Consider these words from *Come Away, My Beloved*:

> How can I give you healing for your body while there is anxiety in your mind? So long as there is dis-ease in your thoughts, there shall be disease in your body. You have need of many things, but one thing in particular you must develop for your own preservation, and that is an absolute confidence in my loving care.
>
> "Come unto Me," it is written, "all ye that labor and are heavy-laden, and I will give you rest" (Matthew 11:28). Only when your mind is at rest can your body build health. Worry is an actively destructive force. Anxiety produces tension, and tension is the road to pain. Fear is devastating to the physical well-being of the body. Anger throws poison into the system that no antibiotic ever can counteract.
>
> Ten minutes of unbridled temper can waste enough strength to do a half-day of wholesome work. Your physical energy is a gift from God, entrusted to you to be employed for His glory. It is a sin to take His gift and dissipate it through the trap doors

of the evil emotions of the disposition.

Look not upon others and condemn them for jeopardizing their health by harmful habits and wasting energies on vain pursuits, while you yourself undermine your health by unworthy emotions, and take time, which by keeping your mind in an attitude of praise and faith, could be constructively employed, but instead you allow this time to be a period of destructive action by entertaining such things as self-pity and remorse and evil-surmisings.[5]

The Pathway to Healing

I notice that the fundamental solution set forth in *Come Away, My Beloved* is "absolute confidence in [God's] loving care." That is the health prescription I am now pursuing in my own life. It strikes me as perfectly logical that someone who doesn't trust God, who allows herself to worry and fret and fuss, will get sick a lot more often than someone whose mind is kept in perfect peace, focusing on the goodness of God. That's just common sense—and it makes medical sense too. Is it a magic cure? Can it prevent all illness? Well, I don't know, but it's got to yield better results than the alternative.

The Bible says that meditating on God's Word can literally bring healing to our bodies. I urge you, even as I urge myself, to prayerfully consider the following passages:

My son, do not forget my teaching,
> but keep my commands in your heart,

---

[5]Roberts, *Come Away, My Beloved.*

for they will prolong your life many years
    and bring you prosperity.
Let love and faithfulness never leave you;
    bind them around your neck,
    write them on the tablet of your heart.
Then you will win favor and a good name
    in the sight of God and man.
Trust in the Lord with all your heart
    and lean not on your own understanding;
in all your ways acknowledge him,
    and he will make your paths straight
Do not be wise in your own eyes;
    fear the Lord and shun evil.
This will bring health to your body
    and nourishment to your bones. (Proverbs 3:1–8)

My son, pay attention to what I say;
    listen closely to my words.
Do not let them out of your sight,
    keep them within your heart;
for they are life to those who find them
    and health to a man's whole body.
Above all else, guard your heart,
    for it is the wellspring of life. (Proverbs 4:20–23)

Remember, I am writing this as a woman who has been sick for twenty years. I am not saying this from a position of strength but from a position of brokenness. I am not quoting these verses "at you" in judgment. I am not advocating one brand of theology over another. (Quite the opposite: I'm sure I've given everyone something to bristle about!) I am sharing with you the answers I am pursuing in my own life: not a formula, not a magic potion for healing, but the pathway to healing.

> *Suffering was not a way of life for Job; it was a valley he passed through.*

The beautiful thing about Job—and for some reason, I had never paid much attention to this part of the story—is that in the end he finally gets "the life he signed up for." His suffering, while intense, represented only a very brief season in his life. His life was *not characterized* by suffering. He was showered with blessings, both before and after his trials. Suffering was *not* a way of life for Job; it was a valley he passed through. The Scripture says we may have to "walk through the valley of the shadow of death" (Psalm 23:4), but it doesn't say we have to build our homes there.

Perhaps you've heard people say, "The Lord has blessed me with good health." In so saying, I suspect God has also blessed them with a good, balanced perspective. It's a blessing I am eager to receive.

I

Signed

UP FOR

LOVE

CHAPTER EIGHT

I Signed Up for Love

God likes my undivided attention.

I like working out.

We were at an impasse.

Until the splat.

I can't think of any other word to adequately describe what happened on the treadmill that day.

S-P-L-A-T

For as long as I can remember, I've been obsessed with the size of my thighs. They don't seem to belong to me. I'm convinced they belong to someone else but have shown up and attached themselves just above my nice little calves. Now they are clinging to me like a lost child in a department store. I keep trying to tell them, "I am not your real mother. You better go find her." But they keep clinging. They stare back at me from every dressing room mirror. They wait for me each morning when I awake, defying me to conquer them.

Like many women, I have purchased every pill and potion that promised to serve as my ally in this all-important War on Thighs. I have tried every gadget and exercise scheme on the market. I have spent hours in the gym. I have consumed countless bottles of the "48-hour miracle diet" guaranteed to take off ten pounds in a weekend. I even tried to enlist God's help by enrolling in a Christian weight-loss program. Hey, I was willing to put in the effort. It wasn't like I was sitting on the couch crying, "God, make me a salad with low-fat dressing and bring it in here." I was doing my part; he just needed to do his part to melt the fat away. But the thighs haven't budged an inch. No, not even an inch. Maybe you can relate!

Anyway, back to the splat. So there I was on the treadmill at the gym, running furiously. Then I noticed that a friend of mine entered the gym. I turned my head around and called out to get her attention. I then attempted to convince her to come run alongside me so we could "spur one another on toward love and good deeds." (See how scriptural I am.) Unfortunately for me, turning around was a bad move. I got distracted. And in a graceless moment of sheer humiliation, I fell flat on my face in the middle of the gym, right there in the midst of all the athletes with their firm bodies.

I could barely walk for the next few days. I had huge scabs on my legs for weeks, and even now, many months later, the scars on my knees remain visible. The fall forced me to stop my frantic running, and in the process, I was also forced to confront the truth about what was going on inside of me. It was painful . . . but ultimately, healing.

Am I Lovable?

A male friend recently asked me what all of the female obsession with body image was about. He failed to see the link between personal appearance and love. So I tried to explain it to him. It was one of those "men are from Mars" moments. He just couldn't see the connection! His exact words were, "What does working out at the gym have to do with LOVE?" In his mind, the perfect female body might grab a man's attention. But grabbing attention and getting love are two completely different things. Men understand that; women don't. That's why women do all kinds of crazy things to themselves in search of a man's love.

> *Grabbing attention and getting love are two completely different things.*

Unfortunately, many of us are striving after an ideal that doesn't exist. When Michelle Pfeiffer appeared on the front cover of the December 1990 issue of *Esquire* magazine, countless women surely gazed at her photo and asked themselves, "Why can't I look like her?" But the truth is Michelle Pfeiffer doesn't even look like that . . . not until the photo finish company performs a little magic. Here's the invoice Scott Associates, Inc., of New York sent to *Esquire*:

DATE: 11 October 1990

CLIENT: *Esquire*/T. Koppel

PRODUCT: December Cover/Michelle Pfeiffer

DESCRIPTION: Retouching 1 dye transfer two-piece strip of Michelle Pfeiffer in red dress. Clean up complexion, soften eye lines, soften smile line, add color to lips, trim chin, remove neck lines, soften line under ear lobe, add highlights to earrings, add blush to cheek, clean up neck line, remove stray hair, remove hair strands on dress, adjust color and add hair on top of head, add dress on side to create better line, add dress on shoulder, clean up and smooth dress folds under arm and create one seam image on right side.

TOTAL: $1,525.00[1]

> *The obsessive pursuit of perfection is not reasonable—and it will never bring us the love we desire.*

And we wonder why WE don't look like the women on the cover of magazines! I do think God wants us to take reasonable care of our bodies. After all, it is the only living sacrifice we have to offer him, and the Scripture does say physical training is beneficial (Romans 12:1; 1 Corinthians 9:24–27; and 1 Timothy 4:8). But the obsessive pursuit of perfection is not reasonable—and it will never bring us the love we desire.

At the end of the day it's not beauty and physical fitness that we really want. What we really want is someone to love us. And we think that means we have to make ourselves lovable. But love isn't love if you have to earn it. Real love—God's love—is unconditional.

[1]Duffy Robbins, *It's How You Play the Game* (Wheaton, Ill.: Scripture Press Publications, 1991).

He even loves women with cellulite. In fact, his Word says we are fearfully and wonderfully made, just the way we are. We don't need to change a thing to be lovable.

> For you created my inmost being;
> you knit me together in my mother's womb.
> I praise you because I am fearfully
> and wonderfully made;
> your works are wonderful,
> I know that full well.
> My frame was not hidden from you
> when I was made in the secret place.
> When I was woven together in the depths of the earth,
> your eyes saw my unformed body. (Psalm 139:13–16)

Of Kids, Friends, and Animals

I think what God wanted to say to me—and what I was finally able to hear once he had my undivided attention—is that there are different kinds of love. And I was pursuing the wrong kind. Around this time, my children and I were sitting on the couch one evening. Tara looked up from my lap and said, "Mommy, you're the bestest pillow in the world." I don't think she could have said that with as much conviction to a thin-thighed mommy. I'll bet your children would say the same.

I'll also bet you have girl friends who love you to pieces, even when you can't fit into the size you'd really like to wear. I suspect some of them may actually like you better with a little meat on your bones.

If you happen to have a dog, you've probably noticed how much it loves you. Even when you haven't brushed your teeth or combed your hair, it's still happy to see you. When I come home from a trip to the grocery store, my dogs are so excited you'd think I was returning from 180 days around the world. My chickens and goats seem fond of me, too. Some might say it's just because I feed them. Nevertheless, lately I'm finding great delight in how happy they are to see me, despite my physical shortcomings. Our donkey doesn't care for me . . . but you can't win them all, now, can you?

Da Bucket Lady

I'd like to write a book called *Confessions of a Recovering Bucket Lady,* but my publisher is afraid no one would know what it was about. So let me tell you so you'll know in advance. When the book comes out, I'm sure you'll rush out to buy your copy. At least that's what I plan to tell my publisher.

I firmly believe God deliberately designed all human beings with a hole in our heart the size of the Grand Canyon. It's what Blaise Pascal termed "the God-shaped void"—a place that can only be filled through a personal relationship with our Creator. All of us sense that emptiness within, and we are driven to fill it. But rather than turning to God for fulfillment, as we should, many of us run everywhere else instead. We go out into the world with our little clamoring bucket, and we hand it to the people around us and say,

"Fill me. Fix me. Love me. Make me feel okay." We turn to our parents, our husbands, our children, our friends, our church, our career, expecting them to be to us what only God can be. The result is what I've termed Da Bucket Lady Syndrome.

Da Bucket Lady always thinks the answer to her emptiness is right around the next corner. So she tries to get her bucket filled with accomplishments—both personal and professional. She tries to fill it with the perfect house and the perfect circle of friends. Da Bucket Lady might even look good, because she's just got to have great clothes, the right hairstyle and makeup. She's busy at church, trying to fill her bucket with Christian rituals and church busywork. The reality is she will never rest until that hole is filled . . . and it can never be filled with a bucket.

Jeremiah 2:13 puts it this way: "My people have committed two sins. They have forsaken me, the spring of living water, and have dug their own cisterns, broken cisterns that cannot hold water." Da Bucket Lady tries to fill her life with things that can never satisfy.

Now I'm going to tell you the truth. And if you can get past the fact that it's gonna hurt your feelings, I think you can get set free in a big way before this chapter is through. First, I want to acknowledge that it's entirely possible for you to have people in your life who couldn't care less about you. You hand them the bucket and they toss it aside. But the painful truth is you are probably surrounded by people who are a-bailin' and a-bailin' just as fast as they can. But they are never going to fill that hole. Never.

I got an e-mail the other day from a woman who had heard me

speak recently and was ready to retire as her mother's bailer.[2] (Your bailer is the person you expect to bail and bail until you get your fill.) She said her entire childhood was devoted to filling her mother's bucket: getting straight A's, being the star of the school play, becoming a cheerleader and the class president, etc. Then she worked hard to get into a prestigious university so her mom would have bragging rights. When she graduated, she landed a high-profile, high-paying job and lavished her mom with gifts. She literally drove herself to physical collapse trying to make her mom proud. Trying to fill her mother's bucket. Of course, it was never enough. Her mom was the same unhappy person. She was just an unhappy person with a lot to brag about.

Who do you expect to be your bailer? Let me give you some clues: Who has the ability to make you angrier than anyone else? Who has the power to disappoint you most profoundly? That's your bailer.

Who do you like to brag about? That's your bailer too.

My ministry is to women, but whenever I speak, there's invariably a man or two milling about, running the sound system or organizing the food service, etc. I'll never forget walking out of a conference late one Friday night and hearing a male voice behind me. I turned around and there was this six-foot-something man with tears streaming down his face. "Can I help you?" I asked.

"That woman you were talking about in there? The Bucket

---

[2]I know that "to bail" normally means to remove water from a boat, but in this case we are taking it to mean someone who works with water in an attempt to save or "bail" someone out.

Lady? That's my wife. I love her, but she's killing me. No matter what I do for that woman, it's never enough."

Wow.

If your husband had the opportunity and the courage to follow me out the door . . . do you think we'd have the same conversation? Something to ponder anyway.

Sometimes we women tend to think men aren't quite as smart as we are. Let me tell you, your husband might be a whole lot smarter than you think. Maybe he's spent years and years trying to fill your bucket. But he figured out, long before YOU did, that he was never going to fill that giant chasm in your heart. So he put down the bucket . . . and picked up the remote.

The next time you see your husband staring blankly at the television, just remind yourself: "That's one real smart cookie sitting there."

Here's another clue: If your husband would rather be anywhere else, doing anything else other than be with you, you're probably a Bucket Lady. (Then again, maybe you just married a jerk. One can never tell for sure. But promise me you'll pray about it, okay?)

Will you be smart enough to let your husband off the hook? To let him officially retire as your bailer? Maybe you could buy him a gold watch and host a special ceremony. I'll bet when you stop expecting him to fill you, he might come out of hiding. Then again, he might stay hidden behind that remote—or newspaper, or office work, or golf game—forever. That's okay. You don't need him to fill you anymore.

And I'll tell the single ladies a little secret. Men are born with an internal Bucket Lady Detection Device. They see a Bucket Lady coming at them—I mean a woman who's just trying way too hard to get their attention and win their love—and something inside them starts screaming, "Run for your lives, men! Run for your lives!" Now, they might dally with you before they run for the hills. But you can take it to the bank: He ain't gonna stick around long enough to fill your bucket. The only thing he'll do with your bucket is reach into your heart, pull out what little you've got, and leave you dry.

No doubt you remember the story of the Samaritan woman who meets Jesus at the well. (If not, go read John 4:4–43.) This Bucket Lady had five husbands, plus she was living with another guy, and we can just imagine how many boyfriends were thrown into the mix. Talk about "lookin' for love in all the wrong places, lookin' for love on too many faces"! Now, you would think, if it were possible for a man to fill a woman's bucket, one of these men could have gotten it right if only *by accident*. I mean, at some point, wouldn't the law of averages have to work in her favor?

The problem is, it's not possible.

So she meets up with Jesus. And he tells her the same thing he tells the rest of us Bucket Ladies: "Everyone who drinks this water will be thirsty again, but whoever drinks the water I give him will never thirst. Indeed, the water I give him will become in him a spring of water welling up to eternal life" (John 4:13–14).

Then the story includes a fascinating little detail: "Then, leaving her water jar . . ." (v. 28).

Did you catch that?

She left her bucket at the well!

Once she allowed Jesus to fill that hole in her heart, to place within her that spring of water welling up to eternal life, she didn't need her bucket anymore. She didn't have to live like a Bucket Lady anymore.

You don't have to live like a Bucket Lady anymore either.

> " *You don't have to live like a Bucket Lady anymore.* "

Lavished by His Love

If we were together at a conference right now, I would invite you forward for the "Bucket Surrendering Ceremony." But you can participate right where you are, in your own heart and mind. I want you to bring to your mind a picture of your bailer—that person you expect to fill the emptiness inside of you. That person who has the power to make you angrier than anyone else. The person who can disappoint you more profoundly. Or maybe it's the person you like to brag about. Get a clear picture of that person in your mind. Now imagine him/her standing there with your little bucket in hand, scooping and pouring furiously. Now I want you to imagine yourself reaching toward this person and taking back your bucket. Ask forgiveness and tell him you are letting him off the hook. He (or she) no longer has to keep you satisfied.

Now I want you to picture you and your little bucket walking toward the well where Jesus is seated. Kneel down at his feet. Ask him to fill you to overflowing with the Living Water of the Holy

Spirit. Ask him to so lavish you with his love, his approval, his acceptance that you no longer need to frantically search for love, approval, and acceptance from people. Imagine yourself handing him your bucket and leaving it safely in his care.

You won't need it anymore.

You can return to the well as often as you like. I go there every morning and drink deeply of God's unlimited reservoir of love and acceptance. That's why I describe myself as "in recovery." For some of us, the escape from the Bucket Lady Syndrome will be a day-by-day, moment-by-moment way of life. This is my prayer for you:

> I pray that out of his glorious riches he may strengthen you with power through his Spirit in your inner being, so that Christ may dwell in your hearts through faith. And I pray that you, being rooted and established in love, may have power, together with all the saints, to grasp how wide and long and high and deep is the love of Christ, and to know this love that surpasses knowledge—that you may be filled to the measure of all the fullness of God. (Ephesians 3:16–19)

The amazing thing is once you allow God to fill you something beautiful begins to happen. Not only are you officially a *Recovering Bucket Lady,* who no longer needs people to fill her bucket, you can be one of those rare gems who has something genuinely worthwhile to offer the world. You'll have the love of God shed abroad in your heart, overflowing toward everyone you meet.

Suddenly ministry won't be something you have to add to your list of things to do. It will just be who you are. All you'll have to do is walk into the room, and people will be blessed because you came.

And if that ain't the life you signed up for, I don't know what is.

I

~~Signed~~

UP FOR

THE PERFECT

LITTLE

FAMILY

CHAPTER NINE

I Signed Up for
the Perfect Little Family

My daughter Leah is fascinated by the workings of the universe. It's not unusual for me to find her sitting by the window at night, just staring up at the sky. Earlier this year, she had a school assignment to write *one paragraph* about the planets. She wrote *seven pages* before I told her she had to stop. She then proceeded to draw an elaborate cover for her "report." So you've got the idea, right? Leah loves the night sky.

On November 17, 2001, the comet Tempel-Tuttle swung past the sun for the first time in nearly thirty-five years, creating what is known as the Leonid meteor shower. But Leah and I didn't get to watch the comet together . . . because it happened on the weekend. And she is with her father on the weekends. I called her late in the evening and reminded her to set the alarm clock for 2:00 A.M., just as I was setting mine. I told her I'd call first thing in the morning and we could tell each other how many shooting stars we had counted.

The meteor show was spectacular. As I lay on a blanket in the middle of the night—without Leah by my side—I comforted myself by singing the old Disney tune "Somewhere out there beneath the pale moonlight, someone's thinking of me and loving me tonight." (You remember, right? Sung by Linda Ronstadt?) It was bittersweet.

The next morning was pure bitterness. I called Leah, and the moment she heard my voice, she started sobbing. Her dad was groggy when the alarm went off . . . so he turned it off.

She had missed the meteor shower.

I held my composure through the phone call, but when I hung up, I completely fell apart. I can't remember the last time I cried that hard. A friend was joining me for breakfast and she thought some disaster had befallen my children. When I explained, through tears, what had happened, I don't think she quite "got it." It seemed like a small thing.

And I guess that's what broke my heart. I didn't want a vacation on the French Riviera. I was just an ordinary mom who wanted to share a meteor shower with my daughter. Was that really asking so much of the universe?

When I was expecting my first child, I had the same dreams every new mother has. I never dreamed I would be robbed of such a simple pleasure. I remember when I decided to homeschool. I was so excited I read every book on the market. Then I reread them. Every Monday night I gathered together with a group of home-schooling moms. We called ourselves "The Charlotte Mason Society." We were going to shelter and protect our children. We signed up for double duty, as both mother and teacher, but we knew it would be worth all of the sacrifices. Because we were going to spare them the heartaches we had endured.

I bought dozens of teaching tapes by homeschooling experts and listened to them over and over and over. In my car. In the kitchen. While I went for my daily walk. I attended conferences. Everyone told me the same thing. If I would just sign up for home-schooling, I could have the perfect little family. My kids wouldn't become "worldly," they wouldn't become "secular humanists," they wouldn't go through teenage rebellion. I might even be able to get them to wear matching outfits.

I signed up to have the perfect little family. I did more than sign up, though. I gave it everything I had to give. A neighbor once said to me, "Donna, I've never met anyone who tries as hard as you." My mom tells me the same thing all the time, except she's usually crying when she says it. We even moved our family to a homestead in the mountains, seeking a simpler way of life. I sincerely thought we had a chance to make the cover of *Perfect Homeschooling Family* maga-zine.

But something went wrong. Terribly wrong.

I won't tell you the whole story, but believe me, it was a night-mare. An absolute nightmare. I didn't sign up for it. Now I'm just trying to get past it, by the grace and mercy of God.

So here I am. Trying to piece my little family back together. A patchwork of Mom's house, Dad's house, and heartache like you wouldn't believe. Well, maybe you would believe it. Maybe you've lived through far worse. Divorce is hell. Don't let anyone convince you otherwise. Having said that, let me add a sentence that will blow plenty of people out of the water: Nothing has made me more like Jesus than my divorce. More compassionate. Less inclined to throw stones.

Don't get me wrong. I didn't sign up for divorce and I'm not glad it happened. Having witnessed the excruciating pain my children have endured, I know why God says, "I hate divorce" (Malachi 2:16). We should all hate it. Experts say the pain experienced by children of divorce actually gets *worse* over time. Hard to imagine, but from where I sit, it sure looks true.

I always tell people: If there is any conceivable way to save your marriage, if there is even a shred of love or respect left between you, by all means, stay together for the sake of the children. Get on your knees and beg God for the grace to make the most of whatever you have to work with.

For my part, I keep adding animals, thinking that will alleviate the pain. If not the pain, then at least the loneliness. I was always appalled when I went to someone's house and discovered they allowed a dog indoors. Unthinkable! Guess who now has a German shepherd sleeping in her bedroom? Not only do I feel safer, I'm grateful for the company.

Leah worked all last summer to buy a miniature donkey named Brighty. He served as a great distraction for a while. The empty-nesters who live nearby "gave" Leah a horse: a twenty-two-year-old Arabian–Tennessee Walker named Frisco. Frisco still lives with the Morris family, but he's Leah's horse, and she can ride him whenever she likes. Some days she spends more time over there than over here. I can't say I blame her. Home is a constant reminder of what we've lost.

We're not alone, of course. According to noted Christian psychologist Dr. Neil Clark Warren, "Seventy percent of us have experienced a broken home, either from our parents' or our own failed marriages."[1] So much for the perfect little families we all signed up for.

Which reminds me of an e-mail Tracie Peterson[2] sent me not long ago. She said (I'm paraphrasing here), "Donna, sometimes life is like this. You're walking a narrow path between two walls. Straight ahead is a huge pile of horse manure. What are you going to do? Turn around? Pretend you don't notice the manure? Deny that it's there? Or are you going to press on through, knowing full well how bad it stinks, so you can get to the other side?"

Tracie thought I should press on through. And she thought it might be helpful for me to stand up and say, in a really loud voice: "There are a whole lot of wonderful Christians—people who love the Lord with everything they've got, people who never signed up for horse manure—

> **"**
>
> *Jesus is taking you to green pastures, right beside the still waters.*
>
> **"**

walking between these two walls." So hold your nose and press on through. If people point out that you've got horse manure on your feet, tell them you're going to keep walking forward with Jesus until

---

[1]Candy Williams, "Psychologist offers help in finding your soul mate," *The Tribune-Review,* February 12, 2002.
[2]Bestselling author of Christian fiction.

the smell goes away. He's taking you to green pastures, right beside the still waters, and that ought to solve the problem. Then tell them you're praying they don't get stuck between those two walls.

Not Always What It Seems

It hasn't escaped my kids' notice that our lives have changed dramatically since the divorce. For one thing, matching outfits have entirely lost their appeal for me. I still homeschool, but I canceled my subscription to *Perfect Homeschooling Family* magazine and stopped reading books or listening to tapes that promised A+B would always equal C. I did A+B but I ended up with a great big F anyway. Life doesn't always fit into nice neat little formulas. Bummer. 'Cause I'm quite certain C would have been preferable to F.

> *Life doesn't always fit into nice neat little formulas.*

My children and I still pine for the good ol' days, even though deep in our hearts we all know it was pretty much the bad ol' days, glossed over with some good acting on Mom's part. Sometimes we struggle with envy when we look around and see other people with their seemingly perfect little families.

We were in the car one day when I asked Leah why she hadn't played with Rachel lately. She said she felt weird because Rachel couldn't relate to all the problems we were facing. "Her life is perfect. She's so lucky!" Leah declared.

I couldn't believe what I was hearing. "Don't you know what

she's lived through? Doesn't she talk about it?"

"Talk about what, Mom?"

Let me back up and tell you about Rachel's family, the Cunninghams, because they are among my all-time favorite families. Her parents, Dave and Melanie, have a great marriage. Dave treats Melanie like a queen, and she is truly one of the most sweet-spirited, godly women I've ever known. And I say that knowing her very, very well and having watched her closely in stressful situations. I met them and their two beautiful daughters at a homeschool gathering in the late 1990s. My first thought was, "Now, there's a family who wouldn't know a problem if it walked up and introduced itself." They looked like they'd just stepped off the pages of *Little House on the Prairie*.

Several years passed before I found out just how wrong I was. When I discovered the truth, I was initially stunned. But then it simply reinforced what I've always known: No one knows what people are up against in their private world. That's why we're completely unqualified to pass judgments.

Holding on to your seat? This is the THIRD marriage for both Dave and Melanie. Not second. Third. You'd never guess it, but Dave is not their children's "real" father; their "real" father is missing in action and has been throughout most of the children's lives.

Shortly before their marriage eight years ago, Dave and Melanie both encountered Jesus in a life-changing way. After years spent wandering lost in the wilderness, they'd finally found the way home. They were thrilled about their new life with God and each other. At last they had discovered the life they originally signed up for.

Not quite.

Within a year of his conversion, Dave's prior life caught up with him. He had committed a white-collar crime, and although he was a new man with a new life, he had to pay the price. So he was sent to federal prison. Dave says it was the best five months of his life, even though it was the worst five months of his life. It forced him to get on his knees. It forced him to confront the truth about his life, like how he'd inadvertently signed up for most of his heartache through his own foolish choices (remember chapter 4?). We reap what we sow, forgiveness notwithstanding. It gave him ample time to study his brand-new Bible and to discover that God is far more interested in what's going on inside of us than he is in what's going on around us.

The Cunninghams also found out who their real friends were. Like Mildred, an older woman at the little Baptist church they attend. The first week Dave was in prison, she took out a piece of paper during Sunday school and passed it around for everyone to write him a note of encouragement. She did that every week without fail. Or another man from their church who called Melanie every single day—yes, every single day—to ask if there was anything he or his wife could do to help.

Doesn't it do your heart good when the church gets it right?

The Cunninghams learned a valuable lesson very early in their Christian walk: not to worry about "what the neighbors say" but rather "fix your eyes on Jesus, the author and perfecter of your faith"

(Hebrews 12:2). They learned to focus on keeping their hearts right before God and to let God handle their circumstances. They knew God was doing a mighty work inside their family, even though their family looked like a mess from the outside. Eventually, the inward reality manifested itself to a watching world. As one of those watching, let me tell you, it's beautiful to behold. It gives me hope, knowing God can heal and transform a patchwork family. He is our Redeemer!

> **"**
>
> *God can heal and transform a patchwork family. He is our Redeemer!*
>
> **"**

The Show Must Go On

Many of us get it backward. We ignore the internal reality and focus on outward performance. We're more interested in what the neighbors think than what God thinks. So we push and shove our families around, trying to fit them into a particular mold. I've been guilty of it myself. I'll never forget what I said to my two daughters on Mother's Day several years ago.

I said: "IT'S M-O-T-H-E-R'S D-A-A-A-A-A-Y!"

It's all in the tone of voice, don't you know?

You see, I wanted them to dress up in matching outfits, put matching smiles on their faces, and look adorable at church. I wanted them to "rise up and call me blessed" in such a way that the whole world joined the chorus. At my seminars, I do this funny little skit about Sunday mornings. Maybe you can relate. Let's pretend it's Sunday morning at your house. You hit the snooze button five times, so when you finally roll out of bed, you realize: You're late for church. Now there is a woman who stands in the back of the sanctuary, making a note of everyone who can't get to church on time. You're not gonna end up on her list! I don't think so!

So you leap to your feet and run into your first grader's room. "Wake up, Katie," you say with sweet urgency. "Time to get up for church. Now, don't forget to bring your Bible. Because you know, every time you bring your Bible, you get two Bible bucks. And once you get ten Bible bucks, you get a star on the chart. And I couldn't help but notice that you're falling behind Jenny on the star chart. Let's get going!"

Okay, that went well. Now the frightening part: You have to enter your teenager's room. "Kristi, Kristi, wake up, honey. We're late for church! Hurry up!" She looks at you as through a glass darkly, then scowls. You remember last night's screaming match. Uh-oh. Better make amends quickly. "Listen, Kristi, I know I really lost it over that whole belly-button piercing deal. I shouldn't have said such mean things to you. But listen. Just last week at Sunday school, the Joneses were talking about the sin of body piercing. Now, you know your dad is up for elder! Do you know how many casseroles I've had to cook to get him on the elder board? If people find out our kids are piercing body parts, it could blow the whole deal. Now, cover that up and let's get going!"

Everyone runs around like lunatics, snapping at each other all the while. Then you jump into the car and race to church, cutting people off along the way. "Hey, get out of my way! I'm late for church!" (Of course, what really bugs me is what happens *after* church. Everyone goes out for lunch, prays before the meal with great fanfare—then makes the poor waiter SPLIT THE CHECK. Ugh! I think we could turn the tide in this country if Christians would do their own math in restaurants. But I digress!)

Finally, you make it into the church parking lot. Mom reminds everyone: "Smiles on our faces. This is church." You get out of the car, and behold, the head of the elder board approaches. Mom does her little beauty-pageant wave and says sweetly, "Praise the Lord. You know, this morning in our family devotional time . . ."

Well, you get the idea. It's all about smiling and lying. And we wonder why our kids drop out of church. Gee. Who would have guessed?

T. S. Eliot observed "The last temptation is the final treason: to do the right thing for the wrong reason."[3] If he's right, and I happen to think he is, there are a whole lot of nice polite church ladies out there committing the final treason.

It's not what you do but why you do it that counts.

Again, it's not what you do but why you do it that counts.

It's not what the neighbors *think* is true about your family that matters; it's what your children *know* is true about your family that matters. Even more important than your children's opinion, however, is God's opinion. God looks at your heart. That's either

> " It's not what you do but why you do it that counts. "

---
[3]From his play *Murder in the Cathedral* (1935).

good news or bad news, depending upon how you're living your life. I encourage you—even as I remind myself—to live your life before an Audience of One.

Another one of my favorite passages is 1 Corinthians 4:2–5:

> Now it is required that those who have been given a trust must prove faithful. I care very little if I am judged by you or by any human court; indeed, I do not even judge myself. My conscience is clear, but that does not make me innocent. It is the Lord who judges me. Therefore judge nothing before the appointed time; wait till the Lord comes. He will bring to light what is hidden in darkness and will expose the motives of men's hearts. At that time each will receive his praise from God.

God knows our motives and he will reward us according to what is in our heart, not based upon how well we perform. What would it profit a woman to fool the whole world, smiling and lying the whole way, when her heart isn't right before her God? And why should it matter to a woman if the whole world misunderstands her, misjudges her, underestimates her, if her heart is right before her God?

Getting With the Program

Maybe you're thinking, "Hey, wait a minute, Donna. You're being too hard on us moms. We just want what's best for our kids." On one level, I'm certain that is absolutely true. On a deeper level, I'm not so sure. If we really want what's best for our kids, we'll ask

God to show us. And I just can't imagine God instructing people to push their kids the way I routinely see parents pushing their kids. I could be wrong, of course, but in this particular case, I don't think I am.

I recently read a magazine article about how obsessed Americans are with kids' sports. One particular sentence caught my attention. It said: "The Cold War is over . . . and the East Germans won." Think about it. It applies to many areas, not just sports.

You may think you're just trying to be a good parent, but I'm challenging you to look deeper to see if something else is going on. You're just trying to get little Bobby to soccer practice. Just trying to help Susie get an A on her paper. Just trying to get the family to church on time. But they refuse to get with the program. This may sound unimaginable, but maybe your kids aren't the ones standing in the way of your progress. Maybe God is and He's just using your kids as a roadblock. (Read Numbers 22:4–33 and think about who was really blocking Balaam's path.) Maybe God doesn't want you to get to soccer, softball, gymnastics, and band practice on time. Maybe he doesn't want your kids to "get with the program," and that's why their hearts aren't in it.

> *God knows our motives and he will reward us according to what is in our heart, not based upon how well we perform.*

You know the program I'm talking about. The one where we push little Jason into the right preschool so he can learn to read early and get a head start so he can do well in grade school so they'll put him in all the advanced classes in high school so everyone will know "what a marvelous job we've done with him." Meanwhile, we want him to excel in sports so he can make the varsity team and catch the attention of college scouts so he can get into a top-notch university so he can get a great job so he can live in a beautiful house and buy nice things so he can die with a lot of stuff.

Da Bucket Lady Revisited

In a very real sense, it all comes back to Da Bucket Lady, desperately trying to find someone or something to validate her existence. We feel like we need to justify ourselves and give the world a good reason why it should allow us to take up breathing space on the planet. If only we could "accomplish" something! (More on that in the final chapter.) Our society is obsessed with success, but we're not sure how, as women, we can measure it. I don't meet many women who are still trying to break through the glass ceiling, although I assume they're still out there. But I know many women are working outside their homes just so they can buy more stuff. Of course, that's not the only reason women work outside the home. Some do because God has called them to a particular career or ministry; others because they can't survive on one income; still others, like me, because they are single parents. But I think ya'll know what I'm talking about.

Some women seek a sense of accomplishment and validation through ministry or charity involvement. I've talked with many church leaders, and they are unanimous in concurring with my assessment that one of the major problems in your average church is people entering into ministry for the wrong reason. They aren't in ministry to serve but to get their bucket filled. Why? Because they are not allowing God to fill it and—this is so key—they've given up hope of getting it filled at home. So they run to church with their empty, clamoring buckets. The results are both predictable and inevitable.

My guess is, however, most women reading this book define success according to their relationships. It is said, "Behind every successful man there is a _____ woman." You can fill in the blank based on whatever kind of woman you think it takes. So if your husband is successful, you are successful. Does it follow then, that if your husband is a failure (however you want to define that), you are a failure?

I've had the unfortunate displeasure of meeting women who brag incessantly about their husbands. As I'm sure you've noticed, there's a difference between loving admiration and bragging. It's subtle but unmistakable. During the Gulf War, there was a woman in our neighborhood you couldn't get within a mile of without hearing how her husband was single-handedly making the world safe for democracy. I remember one occasion where she waxed eloquent about her heroic husband—and how he was her ticket to the good life—for nearly an hour. It wouldn't have been too dreadful except there were two widows and three divorced women in the room. Maybe she was just proud of her husband, but I suspect something else was going on. It was her way of saying, "I may not seem wonderful, but imagine how wonderful I must be if *such* a man loves me."

If you're constantly goading your husband on to success, you might stop and ask yourself, why? Why is it so important for him to climb higher and higher, earning more and more money? Is it about him? Or is it about you?

Far more common than women bragging about their husbands is women bragging about their kids. What's that about? Maybe it's about a lot of things, and I don't pretend to know the motives of every bragging mom in the world. But I do think there's tremendous pressure on Christian women to make their kids turn out right. I've felt the pressure; I've given in to the pressure.

Is there something inherently wicked about kids playing soccer? Of course not! The question, again, isn't "What are you doing?" but "Why are you doing it?" If you take your kids to soccer practice because their bodies are the temple of the Holy Spirit and need to be exercised, that's wonderful. Or because they love playing soccer, that's wonderful. If you're doing it because Doreen's kids are playing soccer or because your child has a chance at a soccer scholarship, maybe you need to think twice about it.

The Blessing Isn't for Sale

Have I left you wondering, "Doesn't anybody get it right? Doesn't anyone have the perfect little family we all signed up for?" Actually, I have seen a few, but they are NOT first generation Christians.[4] They are almost invariably people who were raised in genuine Christian homes—as opposed to "smiling and lying" Christian homes—where a premium was placed on loving God and loving people. Often they represent many generations of devout believers.

I'll never forget sharing the platform with a beautiful young woman who gave her testimony and sang just before I was scheduled to speak. Typically, she spoke to teenage girls, but this was a group comprised mostly of women in their thirties and beyond. However, she did not alter her message to suit the audience, which was initially very unfortunate . . . but ultimately, powerful.

She shared about her life growing up in an incredibly warm, loving Christian home—how her father always cherished her and how easy that made it for her to embrace the love of a heavenly Father. She told about a special dinner date she had with her father, early in her teen years, and how she pledged to save herself for marriage. She committed herself never even to date but to hold out for God's perfect choice and to pursue the path of courtship.

And because she chose not to waste her time on the dating scene, she was able to focus on her studies and gain admittance to a prestigious university. Her unspoiled beauty and purity won the attention of the judges at the Miss America pageant, where she was a finalist. God gifted her with an extraordinary singing voice, and because she was faithful to cultivate that gift and use it for his glory, she recorded a nationally released CD before turning twenty-two.

---

[4]For more on the topic of first generation Christians, please refer to my previous book *Standing Firm*.

Shortly thereafter, God did indeed reward her faithfulness by bringing along a handsome, wealthy professional athlete from a wonderful Christian home who fell madly in love with her. When she shared the story of his marriage proposal, it was like something out of a fairy tale. He sang to her at the wedding, and he too had such an extraordinary voice that a music company executive, who was on hand for the ceremony, offered him a contract on the spot.

In between these amazing stories of God's abundant blessings, she sang like an angel. When the women finally realized "the other shoe" was never going to drop, many of them were visibly shaken. The brightness and beauty of her life in contrast to the darkness they had endured was overwhelming. When she finished, the pain in the audience was palpable. I begged God to give me a word for these women. And did he ever! I picked up the microphone and simply said, "Someday, I want my granddaughter to stand on a stage and tell that *exact same story*. Don't you?"

The audience thundered.

They suddenly got it.

This beautiful young woman's life story was not a message for them; it was a message for their descendants. It was not a word concerning what their lives *should have been* but what their descendants' lives *could be*.

Did you know the Bible says blessings pass from generation to generation? Look:

> I, the Lord your God, am a jealous God, punishing the children for the sin of the fathers to the third and fourth generation

of those who hate me, but showing love to a thousand generations of those who love me and keep my commandments. (Exo-
dus 20:5–6)

A thousand generations? A thousand generations! I'm not one to
shout "Hallelujah," but here it comes: H-A-L-L-E-L-U-J-A-H! I've got
a promise from the God of the universe right there in black and
white. He says he will show love to a thousand generations of my
children if I love him and keep his commands.

Wow. That works for me!

I believe God showed me something very powerful about my
family and the spiritual heritage he is calling me to labor toward—
not for me, not for the neighbors—for my children:

Blessed is the [woman] who fears the Lord,
who finds great delight in his commands.
[Her] children will be mighty in the land;
the generation of the upright will be blessed.
(Psalm 112:1–2)

Here's what God spoke to my heart: "You thought you could buy
my blessing with a formula. With your A+B . You thought you could
get what 'they' got if you worked hard enough and wrestled with
me long enough. My blessing is not for sale, and it can't be
demanded from me. It is a gift. A gift I give to your children as a
reward for your obedience." I have finally come to grips with the
fact that I will never personally experience "the life I signed up for."
There's already been too much heartache for me. But I believe my

children—and especially my grandchildren—will be mighty in the land. They will tell stories of God's abundant blessings that will make people tremble. That awareness sets me far down the road to hope and healing!

It's not exactly what I signed up for . . . but I'll take it!

I Signed

UP TO

MAKE A

DIFFERENCE

CHAPTER TEN

I Signed Up to Make a Difference

Recently I visited the campus of Wheaton College and toured the Billy Graham museum. What an incredibly moving experience it was to survey his life and ponder how mightily one person can be used in the kingdom of God. What a difference one man can make! My editor, Steve Laube, was with me. Just before entering the museum we had finished an "important" discussion about how I could sell more books. When we turned the corner into the first display area, I suddenly felt incredibly small, not to mention small-minded, so I turned to him and said, "Please smack me upside my head! What was I thinking? It's about faithfulness! It's not about how many books I sell or how many people attend my conferences! It's about faithfulness! I just want to be faithful!"

He solemnly promised to remind me of this insight on a routine basis in the future. We continued our tour of the museum, continued standing in awe of this giant of the faith. As we walked out the door, Steve turned to me and said, "There was a woman in our church who continuously prayed through the church directory, one family at a time. Every once in a while, we'd get a note from her saying, 'I prayed for you today.' She did it for years. She was faithful too, Donna, even though no one is going to build a museum in her honor."

It reminded me of a woman at a church I once attended. She had volunteered in the nursery for twenty-three years. Twenty-three years of caring for other people's two-year-olds so they could enjoy the morning worship. I doubt they'll ever erect a statue of her. The most faithful servant I've ever personally known was Dr. William Miller. In 1919 he sailed for Persia (now called Iran). He spent the next forty-three years as an itinerant evangelist, journeying from village to village, sharing Christ with the Muslims of that land. In all those years he saw only a small number of converts. He never built a huge ministry, never hosted large crusades. He didn't lead thousands to Christ, but he was faithful.

After he retired and returned to the United States, he continued laboring tirelessly on behalf of Muslims for another forty-plus years: writing books and pamphlets that explained the Gospel in terms they could understand; corresponding with Muslim seekers and converts from around the world; telling everyone who would listen about the desperate need to take the light of Christ to these lost souls. Twice each year, for twenty-nine years, he hosted the Fellowship of Faith for Muslims (FFM) Day of Prayer. He continued hosting the event until he was 101, even though, for most of those years, the event attracted only a small number of die-hard participants. Toward the end of his lifetime the FFM prayer movement began to grow, and it was one of his greatest joys.

He touched my life profoundly—precisely *because* he wasn't "successful" by the world's standards yet he persevered anyway.

He was faithful.

The Measure of Faithfulness

The problem with faithfulness, of course, is that we're not quite sure how to measure it. We think if we're truly faithful, we will automatically be successful. And how do we measure success? By achievement. By the numbers. By crowds and money. By the volume of approval and applause generated. We want tangible proof, for all the world to see, that God is blessing us. But we're back to square one: How do we define blessing?

I took a much-needed break from writing yesterday and spent the day with my friend Kathleen. For the past eight years she has taught a community-wide women's Bible study, sponsored by an Evangelical Free church, hosted at a Southern Baptist church, but attended by women from all denominations, from Catholic to Charismatic. She is an incredibly gifted Bible teacher. Yet the number of women who attend has steadily dwindled in recent years rather than steadily increasing.

Frankly, I hadn't noticed, because when I show up for women's Bible study, I'm glued to my chair. More accurately, God's got me nailed to my chair, if you know what I mean. Since I travel many weekends throughout the year, conducting women's retreats, I often spend Sunday at airports rather than church. So Kathleen's teaching has been a major source of spiritual food for me. I'm always amazed at how God will speak through her exactly what I need to hear on a particular day. I know you've had the same experience with your own pastor or favorite Bible teacher.

I'm quite certain there are dozens of other women who feel the same way about Kathleen's teaching. So is God blessing her ministry, even though the number of women in attendance isn't skyrocketing? Is she successful? Is her life making a difference? She's certainly making a difference in my life.

We all want our lives to count for something. We want to make a difference. But so many of us were taught by the church that the only way to make a difference is to "get it right." If only we could live out the "life everyone signed up for," then people around us would want to become Christians too. That's certainly true. There *are* people God has called to be glorious, shining lights in a dark world, like the beautiful young woman I described in the previous chapter. I know God works through her in a powerful way to inspire other young women to pursue holiness and personal purity. Her life is so blessed, who wouldn't want to be like her?

But since you've chosen to read a book entitled *This Isn't the Life I Signed Up For,* I suspect you're wondering if there is any way an ordinary woman like you can make a difference too. I've got great news for you. Do you know what happens when God takes your mess and adds a little age to it? Watch this:

Mess + age = Message

I often tease the women who've been blessed with great lives. "See that! You didn't make a mess, so you're just getting old. It's us mess makers who've got a message!" Actually, that's not true. We *all* have a message! Some can speak a message of God's abundant blessing. Others, like me, can speak a message of God's abundant mercy. The world needs to hear both messages preached loud and clear.

Philippians 2:14–16 encourages mess makers that we too can be shining lights, but only when we stop complaining about the mess and choose to move forward in search of hope and healing:

> *Some can speak a message of God's abundant blessing. Others, like me, can speak a message of God's abundant mercy.*

Do everything without complaining or arguing, so that you may become blameless and pure, children of God without fault in a crooked and depraved generation, in which you shine like stars in the universe as you hold out the word of life.

I believe our most powerful opportunities for ministry are often borne out of our mistakes, out of our brokenness, out of those things in our lives that we didn't sign up for. Or things we signed up for, out of our own foolishness, but now wish we hadn't. I've shared extensively about ministering out of our "broken places" in my prior books *Living in Absolute Freedom* and *Standing Firm,* so I will not revisit it here. Except to say this: I find it extraordinary that God wants to take the very things we *didn't sign up for* and use them for his glory. I know for certain that he has taken my broken places and made them the centerpiece of my ministry.

Turn and Strengthen Your Brothers

Surely you know the story of Joseph. (If not, read Genesis 37–50.) He didn't sign up to be sold into slavery by his brothers. He didn't sign up to be unjustly imprisoned. He didn't sign up to be forgotten and left rotting in a dungeon. Ultimately, however, God turned his life around, making him a ruler in Egypt and a shining light for all generations. In speaking to his brothers, who had caused him so much pain, he said, "You intended to harm me, but God intended it for good to accomplish what is now being done, the saving of many lives" (Genesis 50:20). Maybe people have intended to harm you; God intends to save many lives through you. Your pain can make a difference. It says in verse 21 that "he reassured them and spoke kindly to them." Having found hope and healing on the other side of brokenness, he was in a position to turn and strengthen his brothers.

> *Our most powerful opportunities for ministry are often borne out of our mistakes, out of our brokenness, out of those things in our lives that we didn't sign up for.*

This is the very thing Jesus instructed Peter to do.

> "Simon, Simon, Satan has asked to sift you as wheat. But I have prayed for you, Simon, that your faith may not fail. And when you have turned back, strengthen your brothers" (Luke 22:31).

Did Jesus promise to stop Satan from picking on Peter? No. Did he say he would prevent Peter from failing? No. Did he tell Peter nothing bad would ever happen to him? No. Quite the contrary. Jesus said, in essence, "You're going to be tested beyond your limits, and you're going to blow it big time. Then you'll probably spend some time beating yourself up about it. But when you're done wallowing in regret, get up and use it for good."

Isn't it amazing that Jesus handpicked Peter, knowing full well in advance every mistake he would ever make? Why? Because he knew that when Peter turned back, he would be in a position to effectively strengthen his brothers. God handpicked you, knowing full well every mistake you would ever make. He's not asking you to live a perfect life. He's asking you to turn and strengthen your brothers. He wants to turn your mess into a message.

The woman who didn't sign up for a painful childhood can turn and strengthen others who've lived through the same pain. She can put her arms around another woman and say, "Listen. It happened to me too. I'm not glad about it, but here's how God got me through to the other side." Or she can make it her mission to spare children from the kind of pain she endured.

> **"**
> *God handpicked you, knowing full well every mistake you would ever make.*
> **"**

Perhaps becoming a child advocate, campaigning for tougher sentences for child abusers. She can teach Sunday school and seek to be a positive force in the life of children. Or maybe she can just reach out to latchkey children in her neighborhood.

The woman who didn't sign up for disappointing relationships can teach others the power of forgiveness, providing support to women who are struggling in their marriages or who've been hurt through divorce or other relational heartache.

The woman who didn't sign up to make foolish choices can serve as living proof that God gives fresh starts. I'll never forget one of the most powerful closing ceremonies I've ever conducted at a women's retreat. A very refined middle-aged woman—a woman who was clearly a pillar in the church—walked up to the microphone and said, "I've been in this church for thirty years, and I've never told any of you this. When I was seventeen years old, I had a child out of wedlock and gave it up for adoption." As tears began streaming down her face, a pregnant teenage girl stood up in the back of the church and walked forward. As they stood there embracing, everyone in the room knew that young woman's life was changed forever. She saw with her own eyes that her mistake didn't have to be the end of the world. The woman standing before her was living proof of hope and healing.

The woman who didn't sign up for disappointment with God—who perhaps has endured personal tragedy—has a unique opportunity to minister hope and healing to those facing a similar crisis. Whether it's a child with birth defects or the premature loss of a loved one, there's no shortage of hurting people who need to be strengthened.

The possibilities are endless. For every heartache known to humankind, there is someone qualified to bring hope and healing because they've already lived through it. As it says in 2 Corinthians 1:3–4:

Praise be to the God and Father of our Lord Jesus Christ, the Father of compassion and the God of all comfort, who comforts us in all our troubles, so that we can comfort those in any trouble with the comfort we ourselves have received from God.

Sincere Faith

My life verse is 2 Corinthians 4:7: "But we have this treasure in jars of clay to show that this all-surpassing power is from God and not from us." I firmly believe the world doesn't need to see how perfect we are; it needs to see how powerful God is. People don't need to see how Christians never have any problems and never make any mistakes; they need to see how God is bigger than our problems and more powerful than our mistakes.

Another of my favorite passages is 2 Corinthians 2:17: "Unlike so many, we do not peddle the word of God for profit. On the contrary, in Christ we speak before God with sincerity, like men sent from God."

In the original Greek, the word *sincerity,* or sincere faith, literally means "without wax." During New Testament times, clay pots were big business. They were like first-century Tupperware—used for hauling and storing everything imaginable. Now, here's the important point. Each jar of clay was handmade, and it was inevitable that there would be some kind of crack or flaw somewhere in it. Everyone knew about the cracks. But since it was big business, the people selling the clay pots would cover the cracks with wax. It was all a game.

In the same way, we have this treasure—the radiance and glory of the living God—but we have it in a jar of clay. Each of us is handmade by God, completely unique. But since we live in a fallen world, where our fellow jars of clay routinely bump into us, some cracks are inevitable. And here's what I want you to grab hold of. Everyone knows about the cracks! So why waste time covering them up?

What's the number one reason non-Christians give for not attending church? "They're all a bunch of hypocrites!" See? They know about the cracks! They know about the wax! They know it's all a game, and they'd rather play something more fun, like golf, on a Sunday morning.

It's time to get real. It's time to strip off the wax and be honest enough to admit we're just jars of clay, like everyone else, and we have our share of cracks. We've faced heartaches and hard times. This isn't the life we signed up for . . . but! Here's the important part: We're finding hope and healing.

That's what we can offer the world. Hope and healing.

Sharing Isn't Spilling

The young pregnant girl mentioned above didn't find hope and healing by looking at perfect church ladies. She found hope and healing when one of those seemingly perfect church ladies had the courage to strip off the wax. Will you have the courage to strip off the layers of wax you've spent years building up?

Now I need to add a word about balance, because I've been

guilty of being out of balance myself. We don't need to share every sordid detail of our life story with everyone we meet. Again, it comes back to why we're doing what we're doing. It benefits no one for you to "spill the beans" to everyone who gets within a mile of you. What are your motives for sharing your broken place? Are you looking for sympathy? Attention? Are you just wanting to "one-up" someone else's heartache? To say, "Oh, yeah, that's nothing! My life is way worse than yours."

One of the wrong motives God recently showed me is that very often I would "expose my cracks" to people *so that* they would make "allowances" for me. I wanted them to say, "Well, poor Donna. Now that we know her full story, we won't expect her to behave appropriately. No matter how outlandish she gets, we'll just excuse her for it." (That way, even though my behavior deserved disapproval, I could still get some approval thanks to the sympathy factor. The Bucket Lady rears her ugly head again!) The only legitimate motive for sharing our pain is to bring hope and healing to others.

Even when our motives are right, we still need to be sensitive to how and where we share. It's taken me a long time to figure out that sharing isn't the same as spilling. Being raw isn't the only way to be real. We must share truth in a way that doesn't defile us, our loved ones, or our listeners. As we listen to God, he'll give us the right words to share at the right time with the right people. He is far more eager to redeem our broken places than we are to have them redeemed.

Jesus said, "If I be lifted up . . . I will draw all men unto me" (John 12:22). If we want to make a difference, we will share our lives in a way that Jesus is lifted up. The punch line of every testimony must be "But God!"

I was in pain, but God . . .

I made foolish choices, but God . . .

I couldn't find my way, but God . . .

It's not about us. It's about God. Remember that, and you're halfway healed.

President Calvin Coolidge once said, "You can't do everything at once, but you can do something at once." Begin today. Allow God to take those things in your life you didn't sign up for and use them for the saving of someone's life. Your life can make a difference!

I leave you with these words of encouragement, posted on my office wall:

> Joy alone is a healer, and you can have it in the darkest hour if you will force your soul to rise to Me in worship and adoration. Bring your sorrow, and watch for the sunrise of the resurrection. Yea, verily there comes always a resurrection—a morning when hope is reborn, and life finds a new beginning. Let his peace flow in you like a river, carrying away all the poison of painful memories and bringing to you a fresh, clear stream of pure life and restoring thoughts. This is not the end. Press on. The goal line is out ahead, and you may yet be a winner in the race of life.[1]

---

[1]Roberts, *Come Away, My Beloved*, 26–27.